To John!

TORNADO
WARNING

By Tamara Hart Heiner

May we never forget!

Tamara Hart Heiner

care of them, giving them $3,000 for expenditures. With this money, they were able to buy a new car. And Justin didn't miss any work.

Even today Doyle is afraid of storms. If it's sunny and there's a chance of bad weather out, she'll fight, she'll need to stay inside she might be hear the storms. It can't be made practical as well.

Haley T has a love/hate relationship with the local news. Before we'll … pick up, knows her voice by how warm she'll sweet, she calls to settle them … primed … the area.

That happens, yet if just a warning on TV, … remember rescued here.

But Haley upset, just got warning going. One note she said not the news couple to reach from the group up … Cutter.

"I hear it's not just a tornado warning," she said. "I went to look …"

"I didn't get the plans," of her … whole conversation and …

"Because she'll find it dangerous to me … near before it kills me?"

… … …

The … get that of the warning when … comes. Except the weather never sounded like a … Haley couldn't hear it sounded like thunder that flows out … building.

But Haley realized that … use … they need the next time another … … … will say tornado when it … or bring another to the scene of a tornado like … that or … at tracks … around her.

Justin Hammel ended up in the cancer in March 2012, just a month shy of the one-year anniversary of the Joplin tornado.

The Divine Household

Today Royel Starks and his fiancée … they … …

TORNADO WARNING

By Tamara Hart Heiner

DANCING LEMUR PRESS, L.L.C.
Pikeville, North Carolina
www.dancinglemurpress.com

Copyright 2014 by By Tamara Hart Heiner
Published by Dancing Lemur Press, L.L.C.
P.O. Box 383, Pikeville, North Carolina, 27863-0383
www.dancinglemurpress.com

ISBN: 9781939844033

Printed in the United States of America

Cover design by C.R.W.

Publisher's Cataloging-in-Publication data

Heiner, Tamara Hart.
    Tornado warning : the extraordinary women of Joplin / By Tamara
Hart Heiner
    p. cm.
    ISBN 978-1-9398440-3-3
1. Tornadoes --Missouri --Joplin. 2. Joplin (Mo.) --Tornado, 2011. 3.
Disaster victims --Joplin (Mo.). 4. Disasters --Psychological aspects. 5.
Women --Joplin (Mo.) I. Title

QC955.5.U6 H45 2013
551.55/3/0977 --dc23
2013951967

*It is difficult to fully express the losses the individuals in
this book experienced when the tornado tore through Joplin.
The interviews I conducted gave me a new perspective on the
magnitude of natural disasters and the amount of recovery, both
physical and emotional, that goes on for years afterwards. This
book is dedicated to all those who have a natural disaster story,
whether they were a victim, or someone who sacrificed their time
and resources to help.*

Acknowledgements

This book would not exist without the people that helped. They were not merely instrumental; they were imperative. As such, I would be remiss without pausing to thank certain people.

First, Steve Runnels from the National Weather Service. When I first contacted him about this idea, he reacted enthusiastically and supportively. The information he provided about the Joplin tornado was critical to the forward of the book. Any errors in the interpretation of the information he gave me are mine and mine alone.

Next, William A. Gallus, professor of Geological and Atmospheric Sciences at Iowa State University deserves my thanks. He donated his time and speciality to help me create the section on tornado safety. The same thanks goes to Roger Edwards, forecaster for the National Weather Service, and Greg Forbes, the tornado expert from The Weather Channel Companies. These men answered my questions out of the goodness of their hearts, with no expectation of anything in return. Yet they gave my book a solidarity and credibility it could not have had otherwise.

Of course, I must thank all of the women who contributed their interviews to the book: Meg Scaggs, "Melinda" Borup, Kayla McMinn, Piper Divine, Penny Jason, Cara Edens, and Nellie Mitchell. In addition, special thanks goes to Michelle Short, who provided the wonderful and amazing cover photography. Words cannot express my gratitude. They put up with my phone calls, my follow-up emails, my next set of follow-up emails... you get the idea. Unfortunately, there wasn't room in the book to include every interview. A special shout-out goes to those whose interviews weren't included: Teri Moore, Daisy Crawford, Morgan Meyer, Diane Humphrey, Tommie K. Ava, and Angel Inthurm.

Finally, all those involved in the preparation of various drafts, including my writer's group. Hillary Sperry, Keli Wright, Mechel Wall, Charity Bradford, and especially Jake Harper, who gave me the fantastic idea to include a countdown until the tornado strike in each chapter heading. That difference, I believe, is what helped me get a publishing contract.

Many others were also involved. Mark Heiner, my personal publicist. Tanya Murray, who helped me get in touch with people in Joplin. Beta readers and storm chasers who read early copies and gave me feedback.

In short, everything this book is is because of other people. There are simply too many people to list, and I'm afraid of forgetting someone. So, let me finalize these acknowledgements with a huge thank you, everyone.

Table of Contents

A Note From the Author

"For the first time in my life I feared uncertainty; I feared death. But worse, I feared for my children." — Name Withheld

Local residents believe that Bella Vista, Arkansas, my hometown, is a protected area. The hills that rise in the land between Bentonville, Arkansas, and Jane, Missouri, prevent strong winds from getting the leverage required to take off.

While this myth provides some sense of security, it's not actually true. Tornadoes can and have occurred in mountainous areas, valleys, and narrow spaces. So while a tornado isn't likely to hit my city, that's not enough for me to consider ignoring a warning. I remember hiding in the bathtub as a small child as we waited out the tornado sirens. My own children will have similar memories. The night of the Joplin tornado, we hovered in the bathtub for hours, watching several different storm heads on my laptop.

With my husband stationed in Fort Leonard Wood, Missouri, it was just me and the children. I thought I was prepared. We set up camp in the downstairs bathroom, and I felt pretty safe. I put my two boys in the bathtub with their blankets and pillows. The baby sat by me on the tile, laying on her changing pad (I'd like to say sleeping, but she definitely was not).

It was when I conducted these interviews and spoke with survivors that I realized, if a tornado had hit my house, sitting in the bathroom might not have been enough.

When my neighbors and I heard about Joplin, a city less than an hour away, we felt an immediate concern for their safety. We consider Joplin a sister city, much like

17

Fayetteville or Rogers—parts of the northwest Arkansas metropolitan area. Relief stations for donations were set up immediately, with volunteers from different church groups across Northwest Arkansas heading up to Joplin to help.

While driving up to Fort Leonard Wood to visit my husband just a few days after the tornado, I tuned the radio to a station out of Joplin. For hours I listened to stories, as well as pleas, to remember Joplin in the next few weeks, few months…a year.

I didn't think much about that plea until late September. I found myself driving through Joplin again, on my way to a book signing near Kansas City. I wondered about Joplin, if people were still helping, if they still remembered. I wondered if there was anything I could do to help.

The idea for this book came close on the heels of those thoughts. I envisioned it serving three purposes: raising funds for Joplin and other tornado-ravaged cities, providing an outlet for those who wanted to tell their story, and helping to ensure the tornado stay in people's memories forever.

I started the project that very weekend. I narrowed it down to a story featuring women who stood stronger than they thought themselves capable, rising to the challenge to persevere in the face of adversity.

The stories recorded have haunted me for weeks. There have been moments when I am in my daughter's room and I hold her to me, and I wonder what I would have done if it had been me. I imagine starting my normal day, not taking advantage of the mundane moments where I could treasure my children or spend a little more time just being grateful for them. I would not have any idea that in a few hours my life would change. No one ever knows when change will come.

These are but a handful of the experiences the people of Joplin had that Sunday night. Every single person in that city has a story they could tell. My hope is that we will not forget what happened in Joplin. As the months and years go by, other tragedies will happen, and the people in this small Missouri town will become less sensational.

And yet the healing for Joplin is far from over; they will never forget.

I have tried to capture the disruption the tornado caused in the lives of the women in this book. I show them living their lives through each hour of the day—being moms, wives, girlfriends, sisters, and daughters. I show them cleaning dishes, going to lunch, gardening, and pursuing hobbies. Then I show how it all changes. The story doesn't end with the tornado. It continues to the cleanup, the search and rescue efforts, and the attempts to salvage personal items from the debris of destroyed homes. It shows the healing in the weeks that followed. It goes on to show the strength of these women and their families, their fears, and their ability to overcome destruction, loss, and death.

I hope I have done them justice.

Foreword

"There are some things that you never forget. You never forget the feeling. It will always be there and it's so hard to describe."
— Kayla McMinn

On May 22, 2011, a supercell of four different tornadoes struck Joplin, Missouri. One hundred and fifty-nine people died as a direct result, and over eleven hundred were injured. More than 7,600 homes and dwellings were destroyed. All of this happened in an area of six square miles as the tornado moved through the city from the south to the east.

Tornadoes occur all over the world, but the majority of them occur in the United States, east of the Rocky Mountains. About 800 are reported every year. A tornado is a "violently rotating column of air" that drops to the ground from a thunderstorm.

The most violent of tornadoes have wind speeds of 250 mph or more. They can stretch up to one mile wide and live for as long as fifty miles. The Joplin tornado had wind speeds of 200 miles per hour, was one mile wide in places, and covered more than twenty-two miles.

Tornadoes stem from thunderstorms, which develop when cold (generally dry) air moves into warm, moist air. Large hail and strong winds are precursors for a tornado.

Sometimes it is not the temperature difference that forms a thunderstorm, but the moisture difference. The warm, dry air moving into the warm, moist air is a common condition in the Central Plain region, such as Kansas and Missouri.

The changing winds and air direction of a thunderstorm creates a horizontal wall of air. This air often spins, or rotates. A funnel cloud forms when the updraft from a thunderstorm tilts this wall vertical rather than horizontal. The rotating continues, and most tornadoes are formed inside this vertical wall.

Tornadoes can be difficult to see when they first form. Often it is the debris and dust that is visible in the twisting vortex, rather than the cloud itself. When one tornado is created, the conditions are right for another to form as well.

Most tornadoes are weak and live less than ten minutes, having wind speeds of only about 100 mph. Only two percent are strong and violent; yet these twisters are responsible for seventy percent of deaths caused by tornadoes.

Tornadoes can occur anywhere, even mountains and lakes, at any time of year.

The Fujita Scale

The Fujita Scale (hence the F in the F-scale rating) was developed by Dr. Theodore Fujita. He envisioned a chart that classified tornadoes by area and intensity. Originally, his categories were:

F0 (Gale)
F1 (Weak)
F2 (Strong)
F3 (Severe)
F4 (Devastating)
F5 (Incredible)[1]

Eventually, these ratings became more scientific, resulting in the following chart:

F NUMBER	FASTEST ¼-MILE (mph)	3 SECOND GUST (mph)
0	40-72	45-78
1	73-112	79-117
2	113-157	118-161
3	158-207	162-209
4	208-260	210-261
5	261-318	262-317

It is interesting to note that the judgment is not based

1   http://www.spc.noaa.gov/efscale/

on measured wind speed, but on the damage caused by the wind. There are twenty-eight damage indicators, starting with the destruction of a small barn at level 1 to the destruction of a softwood tree at level 28, though they aren't necessarily in order of severity. Each level also has a chart to differentiate between the degrees of damage (DOD).[2] Thus, the F-scale is not so much a rating of wind speed as it is of the destructive force of the tornado. So level 4 at DOD 12 (total destruction of a mobile home), would have wind speeds of about 134 miles per hour and would be considered an F2. Level 19 at DOD 10 (significant damage to a ten-story building, estimates wind speeds of 228 miles per hour. This tornado would be an F4. The Joplin Tornado was an F5.

The tornado scale is now called the derived Enhanced F-scale. Hence the tornadoes are measured as EF1, EF2, EF3, EF4, and EF5.

The Joplin Tornado

The four tornadoes were created from two supercell storms. One tornado was an E5, two were rated E4, and one was an E3. An E5 hadn't hit Joplin or the surrounding area since 1925, nearly a century earlier. This tornado was the deadliest to strike in the United States in the modern era. It traveled almost fourteen miles through the Joplin city boundaries. It began at approximately 5:34 p.m. and ended around 6:12 p.m., lasting about thirty-six minutes. Almost 16,000 people were in the direct path of the tornado.

Severe weather and flooding continued in the area for the next three days, all of it a result of the supercell that spawned the E5.

One hundred and fifty-nine people died as a direct result of the tornado, and over eleven hundred were injured. More than 7,600 houses and dwellings were destroyed. All of this happened in an area of six square miles as the tornado moved through the city from the south to the east.

2   http://www.spc.noaa.gov/efscale/ef-scale.html

Contributing Weather Conditions

"A series of complex meteorological events and interactions took place during the afternoon hours of May 22 that eventually resulted in the devastating EF5 tornado."[3] These events were:

1) A 500 millibar jet core at around 55 and 65 knots (or about 63 and 74 miles per hour) remained mostly stationary over the region. The typical jet stream is about 300 millibars strong.

2) The winds over the Joplin area increased by about 50 knots (or about 60 miles per hour).

3) Winds that had been heading south changed directions and increased by about 35 knots (or 40 miles per hour).

4) A weak surface low (or area of low pressure) formed across the most southeast part of Kansas.

5) A dry patch followed on the heels of the surface low and spread out farther than expected across southern Kansas and northern Oklahoma.

6) A slow-moving cold front spread to the north and east of the low.[4]

These six factors then led to three more problems which created a triangular effect: Winds increased to 60 knots. Moisture pooled in the southeastern area of Missouri. Weather temperature all day Sunday was in the 80s, hotter than what had been forecast, which increased the Convective Available Potential Energy (CAPE).

Hodographs, or diagrams that give a visual representation of a body of air, revealed the classic sickle shape that indicates an increase in tornado potential. The supercell showed a definite eastward movement.

A series of storm mergers occurred half an hour before the Joplin tornado developed. At first, the supercells moved in a northeast direction. But radar operators noted that at least one of the cells was making a gradual right turn. This

3   "Joplin Tornado and Severe/Hydro Event." National Weather Service.
4   ibid.

observation would prove critical for the advanced warning that Joplin received.

Two more storm cells formed and interacted with the (already mentioned) supercell. It developed a mesocyclone that prompted the first warning in Jasper County. A third storm developed and interacted with the ones in the north. This last storm developed quickly and became the dominant cell. It was this cell that prompted the first Tornado Warning for Joplin at 5:17 p.m.

At this point the radar operator made a judgment call: he opted to send out the warning using the WarnGen system instead of the Pathcast. The difference was that with the WarnGen system, the warning went out to all cities and towns that could possibly be in the vicinity of the tornado, as opposed to the Pathcast, which would calculate the direct path of the tornado and create the warning for those in the direct trajectory. Since the tornado proved to be unpredictable, more than once changing directions and speeds, his decision likely saved numerous lives.

Two more storm mergers occurred after the Joplin warning was issued. The first merger increased the wind speed to 100 knots. The second merger brought the water, creating the rain-wrapped vortex of the Joplin tornado. This violent storm was now in the Joplin city limits.

The tornado developed very rapidly, with intensity increasing in seconds. The reasons for this are unclear, though research is being conducted.

Timeline

Weather officials watched the storm develop throughout the weekend. The first indication of a storm began at 2:30 a.m. on Friday. At that time, the probability for a super storm was a "slight risk." A few hours later, at 5:30 a.m., that had changed to a potential for severe or strong Sunday storms.

That expectation held steady over Friday and Saturday. By Sunday morning near 1:00 a.m., weather officials discussed the 10% probability of severe and isolated tornadoes in the area. By 5:12 a.m., the risk upgraded to "limited."

By 10:00 a.m. on Sunday, the possibility of supercells was mentioned. The risk of tornadoes was expected to go up as the evening progressed. At 11:31 a.m., the risk went from "limited" to "elevated," based on the weather patterns that meteorologists were noting for the area.

Storms began forming between 2:00 and 3:00 p.m. that afternoon in Kansas and Oklahoma.

A little after 1:00 p.m. on Sunday, May 22, the Storm Prediction Center (SPC) noted the convective pattern, or convective available potential energy (CAPE). The development of cumulus clouds along the dry patch indicated an eruption of intense supercells. The instability of the atmosphere created the right mixture for a tornado to form. SPC scheduled a conference call to discuss the possibility of a tornado, which was higher than previously expected, but still not probable. The biggest expected threat was large hail. Even so, the possibility of a tornado required a Tornado Watch, which was issued at 1:30 p.m.

The first thunderstorms of the day formed in front of the dry line of Kansas and Oklahoma by 3:00 p.m. A warm jet stream blew into the area, auditing the formation of thunderstorms. The storms quickly developed the characteristics of a supercell: low and mid-level moisture with a lot of precipitation, as much as one and a half inches. Wind fields were only slightly higher than the thunderstorms. The storms interacted and merged together in the manner customary of a supercell. Hail ranging from golf ball-sized to baseball-sized pummeled the area. The storm quickly became severe, prompting Severe Thunderstorm Warnings from the Weather Forecast Office (WFO) in Springfield.

"As severe storms moved east, forecasters became increasingly concerned about their tornado potential and issued the first Tornado Warnings of the day at 4:25 p.m.

and 4:51 p.m. for portions of Cherokee and Crawford Counties in southeast Kansas, west of Joplin."[5] This initiated a conversation with Jasper County about the supercell in southeast Kansas. At 5:09 p.m., the Tornado Warning for Jasper County was issued.

At this point things quickly picked up speed. The Joplin weather tower was notified at 5:15 p.m. The warning was valid until 6 p.m., with an additional notice that there might be more than one tornado cell moving across Jasper County.

People in Joplin began calling in reports of hail at 5:34 p.m. At the same time, a tornado moving toward Joplin at twenty-five miles per hour from Galena, Kansas, was spotted. "The first indication of a confirmed tornado was issued via another Severe Weather Statement at 5:39 p.m. CDT that stated, 'At 5:34 p.m. CDT...trained weather spotters reported a tornado near Galena' and that 'This storm is moving into the city of Joplin.'"[6] The tornado first touched down at the intersection of JJ Highway and Newman Road, just outside Joplin. It intensified and gain E5 status by the time it entered the Webb City limits.

At 5:41 p.m., the tornado entered Joplin.

LSR (Local Storm Report) immediately communicated numerous power flashes, presumably caused by the tornado as it blew out transformers and tore up electrical lines.

By 5:46 p.m., the tornado had already inflicted great damage. The vortex maintained E5 status for most of the fourteen miles it traveled through Joplin. Reports came in of collapsed housing structures and damage to Range Line, 22nd, 13th, and Blackcat Road. The reports kept coming, and the details were grim. By 6:02 p.m., LSR reported that a tornado had blown through I-44 between markers 10 and 12, knocking more than twenty semi-trailer trucks and cars off the interstate. "All interstate signs" were "gone

5   ibid
6   ibid

and damaged."[7] The force of wind required to knock semi trucks off the highway and twist and destroy pieces of sheet metal is nearly unfathomable.

As the tornado continued moving east, Severe Weather Service (SVS) issued a statement that "this storm has a history of producing a large damaging tornado in Joplin Missouri."[8]

The storm pushed its way through Joplin and continued into Diamond, Missouri, where it dropped to an E1 status. By the time the tornado lifted outside of Duenweg, Missouri, it had traveled twenty-two miles.

The damage was done. A storm that took days to develop eradicated entire sections of Joplin within minutes.

The National Weather Service jumped into action. Six members were on staff during the tornado, with a seventh arriving midway through the event. As the damage reports came in, staff notified management and requested backup. Management arrived and quickly began the task of organizing rescue and cleanup operations.

Public Response to the Tornado

The tornado did not catch the city of Joplin by surprise. "Despite being focused mainly on very large hail as the primary severe weather threat prior to thunderstorm development, warning forecasters did an outstanding job of recognizing the tornado potential of the storm that moved through Joplin and issued an accurate Tornado Warning with sufficient lead time for people to take life-saving action."[9] Twenty-four minutes before the tornado touched down in Joplin, news officials started sounding the sirens. Sixty-four Severe Weather Warnings and thirty-six Tornado and Severe Thunderstorm Warnings were issued.

The death toll seemed especially high, considering the advanced notice. This could have been because "the

7   ibid
8   ibid
9   ibid

tornado developed rapidly on the southwestern outskirts of a densely populated area and had moved through much of the city before the size and violence of the tornado was apparent to warning forecasters. Thus, they did not issue a Severe Weather Statement with a Tornado Emergency headline for Joplin proper."[10]

The warnings were issues via television and radio, government and weather websites, two separate tornado sirens, text messages, posts on Facebook, and transmissions over the weather radio. Additional unofficial warnings came from direct observation of the weather, and from family, friends, and neighbors who commented on the warnings.

In spite of these many warnings and precautions, some people were still caught unaware, resulting in an unfortunate number of deaths. The Joplin tornado was the first to have caused over 100 deaths since the 1953 tornado in Flint, Michigan. Reasons for this could be:

1) The tornado was almost a mile wide, with winds of 200 miles per hour.

2) The tornado didn't always move in one direction, and often changed speeds.

The Weather Forecast Office scanned the tornado every five minutes to ascertain the size of the event. Because of the speed of the tornado, however, it had often completely altered course by the time a next scan occurred, leaving weather operators scrambling to project its path. The WFO is considering ways to increase the scan to one-minute intervals.

3) Insufficient available shelter.

Most people who took shelter did so in appropriate places, or the best available to them, such as bathrooms, interior closets, basements, and storms shelters. Unfortunately, belowground shelters weren't common, and many people had no safe place to go. Early assessments indicated that more than 50% of fatalities occurred in the home. While an

10   ibid

estimated 30% of deaths occurred at local businesses, the actions of employees saved the lives of many patrons.

4) A varied response to the warning.

While many people heard the sirens or were aware of the Tornado Warnings, many didn't believe them. Some didn't take any action at all. Those who did often had no place to go, and sought shelter in hallways and bathrooms. Many people chose to wait and see, relying on their own ability to "sense" danger before seeking cover. This is evident even in some of the interviews you'll read in this book. For some people, it took as many as nine different warnings before they took the threat seriously.

Many people familiar with the spring weather in Southwest Missouri noted that tornado watches and warnings are common. However, these same people didn't feel that Joplin was ever affected by such weather patterns. This is called "optimism bias," where people think the risk for others is higher than for themselves. Somehow, they thought Joplin would always be passed over.

The policy in Joplin is to sound the sirens when a tornado is moving toward the city, or thunderstorm winds are expected to reach seventy-five miles per hour or higher. Once activated, the sirens turn on for three minutes, then turn off. Because there is no way to know which threat the sirens are indicating, many people didn't take them seriously. Also, because the sirens shut off after three minutes, some residents assumed that meant the threat was over.

The sirens had lost credibility in Joplin as being a warning of imminent danger. Because of this, WFO suggests creating a different siren that is only used in immediate emergencies. It would need to be used infrequently, thus dispelling the problem of false alarms and complacency. Joplin's policy is usually to sound one siren for an event. Therefore, when the second siren went off, many residents noted that this was unusual. It helped many to realize the threat was real, and not just another warning.

Some people relied on their own ability to recognize a tornado approach; however, this proved difficult with the Joplin tornado, as it was wrapped in rain. Therefore it looked like a dark cloud rather than a funnel cloud. Many people didn't realize it was a tornado until it was at their doorstep, quite literally, as evidenced in the story of Kayla McMinn.

The WFO recognizes they could have given a better warning. They stated that, "the Severe Weather Statement issued at 5:42 p.m. CDT and Tornado Warning issued at 5:48 p.m. CDT should have been more strongly worded and portrayed a greater sense of urgency." Instead, the statement and warning were worded very much like previous warnings and statements issued that day.

As the tornado moved through Joplin, radio and TV coverage switched to live commentators, and the urgings to "take cover now," along with reports of the devastation already created, prompted most to seek shelter. This sort of warning had a feeling of immediacy and an urgency that forced people to act without delay.

Introduction of Characters

These are the seven women and their families whose account of that fateful day follows:

Cara Edens is an undergraduate student studying veterinary technology and business administration. She has an obsessive-compulsive disorder with cleanliness and germs, and sometimes suffers anxiety attacks about going out in public. She lives in Joplin with her boyfriend Stephen and their two cats. Her parents, sister, and nephew all live close by.

Carmen Borup is a stay-at-home mom with several children in college and several still at home. She loves music and helps out with the high school band whenever she can. Her husband is the cook of the family. He takes great care to prepare gluten-free meals for Carmen, who has Celiac disease.

Kayla McMinn lives with her fiance and two sons in Joplin. She stays home to care for them and her mother-in-law. She enjoys cooking and looks forward to Sunday dinners with her father.

Meg Scaggs is an artist who lives with her husband Sam, their dog, and three small children in Joplin. She loves spending time in her garden, and jogging. She recently retired from Spiva, a community art program. She documents their daily lives through photography, taking pictures on her phone and camera whenever she can.

Nellie Mitchell is an elementary school teacher who lives

in Joplin with her husband. They both enjoy bike riding, and Nellie spends every Sunday in Webb City working on her photography. She's a crafty person who takes pride in her ability to create something with her own two hands.

Penny and Pierre Jason have been married more than sixteen years. They have a quiet life with their dog Bella. Penny's children are all grown, and she frequently visits with her grandchildren who live nearby. Pierre has one daughter from a previous marriage who lives with them.

Piper Divine is a single parent who survived cervical cancer. She's also a full-time student and full-time employee. Her mom lives close by and helps her with her ten-year-old son whenever she can.

Chapter One

Sunday morning, May 22, 2011
Approximately 8 Hours before Tornado Strikes

*"I assume one day I will go an entire day without thinking
about the tornado that destroyed my hometown of Joplin,
Missouri, but even after six months that day has not come."* —
Morgan Meyer

The Scaggs Household
A white wood-frame house with a basement
Less than a mile from the path of destruction

"Hey, guys." Meg Scaggs scooped up her shoulder-length brown hair and greeted her children. Three tiny people looked up from the cabinets where they pulled out bowls and cups in preparation for breakfast. "Anyone hungry?"

"Yes!" they cried in slightly out-of-sync harmony. They bumped and hummed excitedly about the kitchen as she walked to the stove.

Meg smiled to herself, her whole body buzzing with energy. She couldn't remember the last time she'd felt so free and relaxed. Yesterday, Scott graduated from Southern University with his master's degree. After five years as a Marine and two as a student, it was finally over; today they could celebrate.

Scott entered the room, scooped up little Harris, and zoomed him through the kitchen. The baby laughed and squealed.

"Here's the deal, troops!" Scott said. "Everyone must be dressed before they can eat! Let's get clothes on!" He pulled Harris close to him and scrunched up his face. "And you, little man…you need a diaper change."

"Eww!" exclaimed Lizzie, Meg's oldest, pinching her nose.

"Maybe it's your turn?" Scott teased, holding Harris out to her.

She shrieked and flew down the hall.

Meg glanced at the clock above the flattop stove. It was a quarter after seven. Church started in three hours. Did she really feel like bathing the kids and forcing them into Sunday clothes so they could sit quietly for an hour?

Not today. She'd spent yesterday catering to Scott's family and friends. She wanted nothing more than to just enjoy this morning. Tonight she'd groom the kids for dinner with her sister and her dad.

She still had food left over from yesterday's huge brunch, but she felt like making something fresh and new. *Like our new start*, she thought. No more school and no more military.

"Ta-Dah!" Nick, her three-year-old, stomped his feet on the kitchen floor. He struck a dramatic pose and flexed his muscles. "I'm dressed!"

Meg gave him a cursory inspection. The green striped shirt didn't match the plaid shorts at all. She let it slide. "Good job! Shall we put on a movie?"

"Yes!"

The Mitchells
A two-story stone house with a basement
Less than a mile from the path of destruction

Nellie Mitchell stepped out of the shower, the heavy cotton towel she'd thrown over her head wobbling. She reached a hand up to steady it. Where was James? Still sleeping? Retrieving the towel, Nellie poked her head into their bedroom. The ceiling fan above the bed whirred gently, a cool breeze drifting her direction.

"James!" Nellie hissed. She stepped into the room and poked his shoulder. "It's morning!"

With his head buried into the fluffy pillow, he grunted, turning his back on her. He grabbed the handmade quilt covering their oak frame bed, tucking it under his chin.

Not that she begrudged James his rest. He worked in three different departments at Landmark Hospital. If she worked that much, it wouldn't be sleep she needed so much as a retirement home. Giving up, Nellie searched through her clothes dresser for a tank top. After slipping it over her head, she slid into a pair of jeans and her black Nike flip-flops, a must for Sundays.

Nellie left the bedroom door open this time, hoping the noises of breakfast would wake James. Back in the kitchen, she opened the cupboard and set out a box of Banana Nut Crunch, then turned on the coffee maker. Her eyes glazed over as she watched the coffee brew. What did she need to get done before leaving for Webb City? As an art teacher at two elementary schools, Nellie kept her life busy with all things creative: photography, painting, sewing—anything artsy. There might be a chance to tackle a few projects before they left today.

James stumbled into the kitchen in his pajamas, yawning and scratching his chin. "Hi," he greeted.

"Hi," Nellie returned.

He poured himself a bowl of cereal and opened the fridge. "We still going to Webb City?"

Why did he ask that every Sunday? "You know it." Cade, a friend of theirs, had built a darkroom in his basement that Nellie liked to sneak over and use for her photography.

James hauled out the milk and poured some into his bowl. "Okay. What time did you want to leave?"

"I don't know. I've got some medium format pictures to print. They're going to take some time."

"So, like, in about an hour?"

"No. I have some things I'd like to get done here, too." The coffee finished brewing, and she poured herself a mug.

"I need to clean up the house, and there are some projects I want to get to."

James gave a short laugh. "Projects...you? This coming from the girl who built our bed in high school? Don't believe it."

"Make fun of it all you want," Nellie sniffed, though she knew James was as proud of that homemade four-poster bed as she was. "You're the one who married the girl who likes to be hands-on."

He stepped closer, running a hand behind her back and nuzzling the top of her head with his morning scruff. "I like it when you're 'hands on.'"

She shoved him away. "James, not now."

She continued as if he hadn't spoken. "Then we can head out sometime after lunch. All right?"

He wrapped his arms around her. "When do I get some 'me' time?"

Nellie laughed and tried to pry herself loose. "Gross! You need to get cleaned up first!"

"Fine." He stomped off to shower.

Nellie sat down with another mug of coffee and her laptop. She sipped her drink as she checked her blog and Facebook, enjoying the peace of having no deadlines. Nellie loved mornings, savoring her freedom and the invigorating challenge of seeing how much she could accomplish before the rest of the world was even getting started.

The McMinn Family
A single-story house with blue siding
Less than a mile from the path of destruction

The bed bounced slightly, jarring Kayla McMinn awake. Her lips formed a smile, and she knew without opening her eyes that her oldest son, Clark, was awake.

"Daddy!" he squealed, throwing his three-year-old body on top of his father.

Clark woke them every morning, either with loves and

kisses or hair pulling and loud noises. Kayla had to admit she liked the loves and kisses more.

"Ohhh," Justin, her fiancé, groaned. "Is it that time already?"

Kayla chuckled and pulled her straight brown hair into a ponytail. That should discourage Clayton, the baby, from grabbing it. "Yep. Rise and shine." With a big yawn, she headed for the kitchen.

Kayla pulled out a skillet and oiled it for her favorite Sunday breakfast: biscuits and gravy prepared from scratch. Cooking a good meal for her family satisfied her. She mixed the flour and milk, making a mental list of the relatives they would visit later. Justin joined her, preparing baby cereal and milk for little Clayton.

"Where are we going today?" Clark asked, following her to the kitchen.

Kayla knelt to his level and pushed his light hair from his eyes. "Let's see...how about to Grandma's house?"

"Oh, yay!" he said, clapping his hands.

"Yay!" Kayla echoed, clapping her hands also. Her smile grew as she watched her two boys dance around the kitchen. *This is perfect. I wish I could freeze this moment*, she thought, her heart warming at their antics.

"When do we leave?" her fiancé asked.

"I need to call my dad to see what time he's coming over," she said as she went to the counter and fished her pay-as-you-go phone out of her purse. Seeing she was out of minutes, she added, "I'll have to use the neighbor's phone. Why don't you get the kids dressed? Then we'll head out."

"Will do." Justin pulled a chair up to Clayton's highchair.

"Oh, and don't forget to feed the fish." Kayla glanced at the 150-gallon aquarium in the living room. "They look hungry."

"Yes, sir," Justin replied with a salute, earning a giggle from Clark.

TORNADO WARNING

The Jason Residence
A two-story red-brick house with a basement
Less than a mile from the path of destruction

Penny Jason sat down to a breakfast of pancakes and milk and waved at her husband Pierre as he walked down the sidewalk toward the Elk Lodge with their dog. In spite of his heart transplant five years earlier, Pierre still enjoyed the occasional walk outside.

The music on the kitchen radio cut out for the newscaster. "Breezy and warm right now, folks, but we are expecting a thunderhead to move in this evening."

Outside looked misty and green, still too early to indicate what kind of day it would be. The music came back on, and Penny got up to turn it off. She listened to that station all day, almost every day — it was the same station they played at work.

She didn't spend all her time working. She'd recently passed the "sixty" threshold, and family felt more important to her than ever. Penny's grandkids were the light of her life, and thank the Lord all but one lived nearby. Pierre's youngest daughter still lived at home with them, turning Penny gray faster than necessary. Praise God for hair dye.

But today her stepdaughter was at her mom's, and it was just Pierre and Penny.

The front door opened and Pierre stepped back in, Bella bounding past him down the hall. He shook off his wind jacket. Penny watched him over the rim of her mug. He looked great for being in his sixties. Several of her friends teased her about marrying a Denzel Washington lookalike, and although Penny laughed with them, after sixteen years of marriage, she not only appreciated, but was very proud of his appearance.

"Blowing out there," Pierre said, oblivious to her scrutiny. His finger shoved his glasses a little farther up on the bridge of his nose.

Penny stood and put her cup in the sink. "So I noticed.

38

How are you?" She stepped close to him and reached a hand toward his chest, stopping just short of touching him. She knew he hated being babied, but she still worried about his heart.

"Doing great. As always." His words came out clipped, just fast enough to give away his Baltimore upbringing. Penny herself was a Southerner. She praised the Lord she and Pierre lived in Missouri and not back east.

He poured himself a glass of milk and took her spot at the table, throwing some pancakes on a plate. "You going to your mother's after church today?"

"Uh-uh." Penny shook her head. "No, I saw her yesterday." Penny's mother lived in a senior apartment building. Mostly she took care of herself, but Penny checked on her at least three times a week. "I'm getting in the shower. Need anything?"

He raised his mug of coffee. "I'm good."

That was her cue to leave. She leaned over and gave him a kiss on the cheek, then hurried upstairs to the master bath. Penny paused in front of the mirror and flipped on the bright lights so she could examine her image better. The brownish-red dye still covered the roots of her short, spiky hair; no need to reapply today. She took her glasses off and the reflection blurred. Good thing she could shower without perfect sight.

The scent of lavender filled the room as Penny lathered her shampoo. She closed her eyes and let the warm water relax her. With a sigh, she turned off the water and stepped out of the stall.

Pierre had turned on the television in the living room. The sounds of comic relief and dramatic displays of emotion wafted through the closed door. At least it sounded like a sitcom and not a football game.

She shivered in her towel and eyed the soft cotton pajamas on the bathroom floor. Without a second thought, she wiggled out of her towel and pulled them back on. She giggled at herself, putting PJs on after a shower, but why not?

Penny joined Pierre on the couch. Bella lounged at his feet, nibbling on her paws. Pierre hadn't changed out of the T-shirt and sweats he'd worn when he'd taken her for her walk. "We're staying home today. Just you and me and the TV."

Pierre smiled and passed a hand over his shaved head. "Sounds like a plan, Pen."

The Borup Household
A two-story, wood-frame house with a basement
1.5 miles from the path of destruction

Melinda Borup snuggled deeper under the covers and resisted the urge to check her watch. She was up early every day of the week, including Saturday; but this was Sunday, and since church didn't start until one p.m., it was the perfect day to sleep in.

The spot in the bed next to her felt vacant and cold. Melinda reached one hand out just to be sure. David was already up. She rolled herself out of bed and glanced at the mirror as she left the bedroom, looking at the circles under her eyes. One blue eye and one green eye peered back at her — nothing unusual there. At least she didn't look tired.

She took the hardwood steps two at a time and joined her family in the kitchen.

"Oh good, you're up." David shot her a grin over the skillet where he flipped a pancake. "I thought we'd have to eat without you."

"Not!" Melinda's nine-year-old son yelled. "We were going to dog pile you!"

"I believe it." Melinda tousled his hair. "I'm glad I got up, then." She stood on her tiptoes to peer over David's shoulder to see what miracle he'd made for breakfast this time. David was the Martha Stewart of breakfast. "Mmm. What do we have today?"

"Plain ol' bacon and eggs. And pancakes." David turned

40

the burner off and carried the skillet to the table.

"Do we have to go to church?" their youngest boy whined, as he did every Sunday.

"Yes," sixteen-year-old Jessica said, adding the customary eye roll.

David added a pile of pancakes and syrup to the table. He placed a plate of eggs in front of Melinda. "Everyone gather 'round! Time to eat!"

Chairs were hauled out of their places as children piled into them. David sat at the head of the table. Melinda sat to his left and took his hand.

"Jack," he said, addressing their ten-year-old, "say the prayer, please."

The children bowed their heads and joined hands, and Jack blessed the food. Then the normal chaos of serving began.

"Do you have any meetings at church today?" Melinda asked as she stabbed her eggs. She had Celiac disease, a gluten intolerance, and couldn't eat pancakes, among other things. She glanced at David.

He shook his head and chugged a glass of milk. "No. Why? You have plans?"

"It's the high school graduation today, remember?" David and Melinda didn't have any kids graduating this year, but their oldest son was playing in the band. "I have to pick Richard up after he plays." Richard would be riding to graduation with some girls from church, but he needed a ride home afterward.

"Oh, right. Not a problem."

Melinda nodded as she rose. "Great. Finish up, guys! We have to clean this kitchen before we leave!" She placed her empty plate in the kitchen sink, then opened the cupboard and pulled out the special, gluten-free loaf of bread she took to church every Sunday so she and her son could take the sacrament with everyone else.

41

TORNADO WARNING

The Divine Household
A single-story beige bungalow
1.5 miles from path of destruction

Piper Divine woke up with a start. She lay in bed wondering why it was so quiet before remembering this Sunday was her ex's turn to have their son. Piper slipped on her glasses and used the remote to power on the TV. No nine-year-old boy demanding his breakfast meant she could take her time getting ready, watch the news for hours, or get online without sharing the computer. Laziness urged her to close her eyes and go back to sleep, but she had things to do today. Of course she missed her son, but that didn't mean she wouldn't take advantage of his absence!

Piper took a quick shower, wincing as she stepped out. "Ouch." She'd just gotten a new tattoo on her foot, and it still hurt. She examined the flowers and teal survivor ribbon for cervical cancer and wiggled her toes until the pain subsided.

Refreshed, Piper ran a comb through her hair. She usually straightened it, but today was a lazy day, which meant she couldn't be bothered with her straightener. She pulled on a pair of Capri pants so that the leg wouldn't brush against her tattoo, and pulled on a tank top. Already the early morning weather felt warm, foretelling a hot day.

Cara Edens' Home
Third story of a multi-level, brick apartment complex
5 miles from the path of destruction

Cara Edens hated being up so early, but Stephen was covering for a coworker today. She made his lunch whenever possible, and she wouldn't skip today just because she'd been up late partying at the graduation for Crowder College. She turned on the sink and washed her hands. She got a good lather up and scraped her fingernails for thirty seconds before rinsing with hot water.

42

Hands now clean, she poured instant oatmeal into a bowl and nuked it for Stephen. His blue lunch cooler sat on top of the fridge. Cara pulled it down, then prepared a sandwich and added a bag of chips. She sealed the plastic baggies and wiped them with a Clorox wipe. Cara did the same to the tops of two soda cans, not minding the extra work to make sure Stephen's lunch was perfect. She couldn't even imagine the filth he came into contact with, working on all those cars. Ugh. The least she could do was guarantee a sanitized lunch.

"Thanks." Fully dressed in his dark blue Walmart uniform, Stephen sauntered into the kitchen and paused at the counter. He scooted his oatmeal in front of him before turning on the TV. Country Music Television blinked on the small countertop screen, the same channel as always.

Stephen finished his food and dumped the bowl in the sink. "I'll call you when I get to work."

Cara opened the front door, hugging her shoulders. The sun peeked over the horizon, but the morning air was crisp and cool. "Have an awesome day."

He patted down his pockets. Cara knew he was checking for his wallet, cell phone, keys, and work equipment. "All there?" she asked.

"Got it." He leaned over and kissed her. "Have an awesome day too. I love you."

"Love you too." Cara watched him take the stairs two at a time down to his car, and then she let out a big yawn. The adrenaline that propelled her from her bed and helped her get Stephen's lunch ready for work had faded. She changed the television channel and listened to the news.

"We can expect some rain tonight," the forecaster said.

Cara glanced outside. The sun shone brightly through the trees, which swayed gently in the breeze. The weather was never right. Rolling her eyes, she switched the channel to a Lifetime movie.

43

Chapter Two

Sunday midday, May 22, 2011
Approximately 5 Hours Before Tornado Hits

"Many have described the storm as the sound of a train...to us it sounded more like jet engines...hundreds of them." — Diane Humphrey

The Jason Residence

Penny's books lay on the coffee table in front of her, beckoning her to enter the written world of fiction. She tried to ignore them and pay attention to the crime show Pierre had on the television. She and Pierre both liked mysteries, thrillers, and cop shows. Now that it was summer, all the shows were in reruns until the seasons started up again. She resisted the impulse to pick up a book. Once she started reading, it would be difficult to stop.

She took another bite of her sandwich, but as the cop on TV shot a perpetrator, Penny's eyes wandered again to the table, where she had both the newest Stephanie Plum and J.B. Robb books. Penny had all sixteen of the Stephanie Plum books. She loved the hilarious main character, especially when the woman blew things up. Almost against her will, her hand shot out and plucked up the novel.

Pierre stopped her, taking her hand and examining her fingers. "You're not wearing your wedding ring."

"Oh." Penny slid out of his grip. "The stone fell out. It's upstairs in my jewelry box. I'll get it fixed next week."

"As long as you don't lose it."

"I won't." Penny opened her book, hoping the conversation was over.

"We should've gone out for lunch," Pierre's deep voice mumbled around a mouthful of chips.

"Hmm?" Penny glanced up briefly from Stephanie's latest adventure and shook her head. "No. There's plenty of food here." Pierre had done the shopping yesterday, as well as the laundry and any other housework. Penny had no idea why he loved doing that stuff, but she thanked the heavens he did.

Pierre's only response was a grunt, but Penny barely noticed. The biggest thing on her mind was whether Stephanie would end up with Joe Morelli or Ranger.

The background noise of the television suddenly turned to static. "Stupid cable," Pierre grumbled, pushing off the couch and moving toward the black box.

Penny didn't bother looking up this time. "It's probably just the wind." Any little weather upset and the cable went out. She tuned out Pierre's efforts to turn it back on. Her book already had her completely engrossed.

The McMinn Family
Grandma Robertson's house: A two-story yellow house
Less than a mile from the path of destruction

Kayla and her fiancé, Justin, headed over to his mom and grandmother's house on Joplin Street. His mom had terminal cancer, and Kayla made it a habit to stop by her house every day to bring a meal. Today she carted along biscuits and gravy.

"What time's your dad coming?" Justin asked.

Kayla shrugged. "He didn't answer. I'll try again when we get home."

They pulled up to her mother-in-law's house and piled out of the car.

"Mom!" Justin called, entering the house.

Kayla put down the baby and followed. She had to slow down so he could hold her hand and toddle along behind.

Grandma Robertson sat in a large chair in front of the

TV, her shrunken frame disappearing into the soft blue cushions. Justin embraced her.

"How are you, Mom? Do you need anything?"

She shook her head. "No, no, I'm fine."

"What about food?" Justin pressed.

"Not hungry."

Kayla kept her eyes on Justin, knowing how hard this was on him. He put on a strong, happy face, but she knew it tore him up to see his mother waste away. Kayla let go of the baby and stepped forward. "Grandma Robertson, we brought lunch for you. Which do you want, spaghetti or tomato soup?"

"I'm not hungry."

"I know, Grandma," Kayla said, resisting a sigh. She went into the kitchen to heat up the food. They'd get his mom to eat even if Kayla had to force-feed her.

Kayla made sure her mother-in-law was eating, but then they had to go. "I'll be back tomorrow, Grandma Robertson."

Just as they were leaving, Justin's older sister Amber arrived.

"Hello!" she called out. "Justin, Kayla, are you here?"

Kayla met her in the entryway. "We were on our way out the door."

Amber flashed a smile. "But you're not gone yet? Can you guys help me move some of my stuff out of the garage?"

"Of course," Justin said, his voice coming from right behind Kayla. "Where are we taking it?"

"My new house." There was no mistaking her pleased tone. "It's just a block from here on Wall Street. I still can't believe they let me buy it!"

"It's rent-to-own, Amber," Kayla said. "Not quite the same."

"It is to me," Amber sniffed. "It's my place."

Kayla followed Justin outside and sent the children to play in the yard. "How can we help?"

Amber opened the garage and gestured for Kayla

46

and Justin to follow her inside. "I've pretty much moved everything except," she pointed, "those things."

Kayla took in the two dressers, the china hutch, the fridge, and the bed. "Oh, so you just have the heavy stuff left."

"Pretty much."

"All yours, babe." Kayla gave her fiancé a smile.

The Mitchells

Nellie began the morning working on photos, then she decided to check on her "project closet" to see if anything needed finishing up.

Big mistake. The closet turned out to be such a disaster that Nellie spent the next two hours sitting on the carpet, trying to organize everything.

"Nellie!" The back door opened, and James stepped into the house. "Whoa. Something blow up in here? Looks like you had a run-in with a tornado."

"Funny." Nellie stood up and pressed her hands against her lower back. "Just cleaning. What's up?"

"Ah, yeah." A big grin spread across James's face, and he held up a small green ball. "Know what this is?"

Nellie squinted. "A giant pea?"

"No. Our first tomato."

Nellie suppressed a giggle. Leave it to James to get a little too excited. "So you killed it?"

He furrowed his brow, looking wounded. "I just wanted to show you."

"You could've left it there," she said, the laughter bubbling up and bursting out of her. "I can walk outside, you know."

He scowled at her, then surveyed the area around her. "So, uh, you ready to leave yet?"

"In a moment." Nellie settled herself back down in the middle of her mess, turning over a few pictures and putting them into piles. "I have to get through this first."

TORNADO WARNING
Cara Edens' Home

Cara made herself a bowl of oatmeal and opened a notebook at the counter. She and Stephen never ate at the table; it was cluttered with homework, mail, and books. The semester might be over, but she already had assignments for the upcoming term. Double majoring in veterinary technology and business administration, Cara had twice as much reading to do.

After a bit of studying, she changed into a pair of ratty sweatpants and made herself a tuna salad. She checked the fridge to make sure Stephen had taken his lunch with him; it wouldn't be the first time he'd left behind what she'd carefully prepared. She hated the thought of him eating food that someone else had touched. He always did sweet things for her; making his lunch was a small way to show her love.

Seeing no sign of the blue lunch box, she relaxed in a chair and munched on her salad. The day was warming up. The windows were still open from the night before, but the air blowing in felt hot and sticky. *Time for AC*, Cara thought. She washed her plate and made the rounds through the house, shutting all the windows. She found the thermostat and made a face. It was almost eighty degrees inside. She cranked the temperature down to seventy-two.

Nothing happened. Cara checked the switches. Everything looked right. She tried turning the temperature down to sixty-eight...still nothing.

Cara groaned and fanned her face. Looked like the AC was broken, *again*.

She took a moment to open the windows and patio door again, then pulled her phone out and called the apartment manager.

"We don't do repairs on the weekend," the man told her. "Unless it's an emergency."

"A broken AC unit is an emergency to me," Cara returned.

"Sorry," he said. "We'll get someone out on Monday."

The wind slammed the patio door. Frustrated, Cara closed the phone. She went back to the patio door and pushed it open. She hit speed dial on her phone and her father answered.

"Dad, my AC is broken. Can you come over and take a look?"

"Sure, Care Bear," he said, his deep voice familiar and comforting to her ears. "Be there in a few. I have to pick up the Pack 'n' Play anyway."

"Oh? Why?"

"We're watching your nephew for your sister tonight, remember?"

The patio door flung itself closed behind her, making Cara jump. She growled and shoved it open again. "Oh, right. Okay. See you soon."

The Divine Household
Cheddar's Family restaurant, a single-story building
1.5 miles from path of destruction

Piper parked her car in front of Cheddar's, a family-friendly sit-down restaurant that served American fare. It was rather windy outside. She threw on her cardigan sweater, glad she'd thought to grab it. Putting on a smile, she ran inside to see Ashley.

Cheddar's was packed. It looked like everyone had come here after church. Piper stepped up to the hostess booth in the noisy, dimly lit lobby. "I'm meeting Ashley Watts."

"Hmm." The hostess scanned her book. "Doesn't look like Ashley's arrived yet."

"Oh. Okay. Put me down for a party of two." She watched the hostess jot down the information, then went back outside to wait.

"Piper!"

Ashley's voice came from the left side of the parking lot. Piper turned to see Ashley waving at her. Her long brown hair hung in perfect waves to her shoulder blades, a short, fitted dress accentuating her curvy figure. Piper had spent weeks helping Ashley plan her wedding, and she hoped Ryan knew what a lucky guy he was.

"Ash!" Piper waved back.

The two friends hugged. Piper pulled back first. "Let me look at you. Married for two weeks now. Well, it must be going good. You look great!"

Ashley laughed. "Do we have a table ready yet?"

"Not yet."

They waited outside for another few minutes before the hostess called Piper's name. Ashley hooked her arm through Piper's and followed the waitress to a window booth. Piper ordered a club sandwich with cheddar and broccoli rice.

"I'll have a French dip," Ashley said. "Oh, and can we get some cheese fries to share while we wait?"

"Of course." The waitress nodded and left.

Piper put both hands under her chin and leaned forward. "So. How was the honeymoon?" she teased. Ashley was a teacher and Ryan a fireman, so they hadn't taken a real honeymoon.

"Ha ha. We'll get our chance." The dimple on Ashley's left cheek showed when she smiled.

Piper shook her head. "I can only imagine. But at least you got a new car out of it."

"Yeah!" Ashley's eyes lit up. "You should see it! It's outside!"

"Oh, believe me, you're going to show me."

The waitress brought the cheese fries, and Piper dug in.

"But you've got something new, too," Ashley said, looking mischievous. "Where's that tattoo?"

"Not nearly as exciting as a car." But Piper obliged, slipping her sandal off to show the tattoo.

"Is your foot still hurting?"

Piper wrinkled her nose. "Sometimes, depending on how I step on it."

50

They finished eating and Ashley followed Piper to her car. "I wish you could go shopping with me," she said, waiting while Piper unlocked the car.

"Me too," Piper said. "Though it's probably a good thing my foot's too sore to go. I'm broke."

"Never stopped you before."

"Ha." Piper rolled her eyes. "What stores are you going to?"

"Kohl's, Hobby Lobby…the like. Maybe even Walmart. Mostly just hitting Main Street."

Piper sighed. "Well, think of me. Have fun."

Ashley hugged her again. "I will."

The Borup Household

After fifteen minutes of reading scriptures together, Melinda sent the kids off to do Sunday-appropriate activities. Since it was the Sabbath, they weren't allowed to turn on the television or the computer.

She helped David clean up his gourmet brunch until he nudged her shoulder.

"Isn't it time to get ready? We leave in an hour."

"Right," Melinda muttered. No matter what time church started, getting the kids out the door was a struggle. She crossed her fingers and went into the sitting room. With any luck, they were already dressed.

Her sixteen-year-old daughter stood in the hall bathroom, doing her hair. Melinda left her alone and looked for the younger ones.

"Come on," Melinda said, spotting her youngest son and tugging him upstairs. "I already ironed and laid out your clothes." They climbed the two flights of stairs to the second floor and found the other two boys standing in the room, arguing over who got to take a bath last.

"You haven't bathed yet?" Melinda asked. Of course not. What ten-year-old boy took a bath on his own? "You're all taking one. So let's just get it over with." She ushered the

51

youngest into the bathtub, then hurried back to her and David's master bedroom on the main floor.

Melinda ran a straightener through her hair, glad she'd bathed the night before. She already had a dress picked out for church. Her shoes were the hard part. She tried on several before settling on a pair that worked for her.

She went back upstairs to check on the boys, expecting to find them cleaned and dressed. Instead, the youngest sat naked on the floor playing Pokemon, and the other two had pulled out the Legos and were building a tower.

Melinda closed her eyes and took a deep breath. "Boys! Get in the bath now!"

They took one look at her and knew she meant it. While they bickered in the bathroom, Melinda turned to her youngest.

"Put clothes on," she told him, pointing to the white shirt and tie she'd laid out.

"But I don't want to," he whimpered.

"Put them on!"

"Everything okay up there?" David's voice boomed from downstairs.

"I got it!" Melinda yelled back. She glared at her son. "Now."

The Scaggs Household

Scott helped the kids clean up while Meg changed her clothes. Sun spilled past the blinds in the master bedroom. She peeked outside. Sunny, with a touch of a breeze. She slipped into a sundress and flip flops, imaging the warmth of the sun kissing her shoulders.

The kids had piled the dishes in the sink and Scott helped Nick wipe down the table. Meg opened the windows, letting in the fresh air. She and Scott had bought an AC unit the week before, but it was nice not to need it yet.

"Can we play outside, Mom?" Lizzie asked.

"That sounds like a great idea," Meg said. "I need to

get some weeding done in the garden." After three years of sitting like lumps on logs, her strawberry plants were finally bearing fruit, and she reveled in this huge success. She had the worst black thumb ever. Last year had been an epic failure; not even the hardy mint had survived.

"Yeah, I need to mow the lawn," Scott said. He looked like a different person in jeans and a T-shirt. Such normal clothing, yet Meg wasn't used to seeing him out of military uniform.

Meg let their dog, Ellie, out to play in the yard with the kids. Scott pushed the mower up and down the flat lawn while the kids climbed on the new playground they'd gotten a few months earlier for Christmas. The house sat at the end of a culdesac, giving the Scaggs a triangular yard slightly larger than their neighbors.

Meg weeded around her cucumber bed, then rocked on her heels. She wiped a drop of sweat from her brow with the back of her gloved hand. From here, she could see the leaves of her potato and onion plants flourishing. Meg inhaled deeply, holding it for a moment before letting it out. Being outside and watching her family gave her a sense of contentment. Life had been near perfect before. Now that Scott had a new degree under his belt, the future felt ripe with financial promise.

And just in time. This past week Meg had told her boss she wanted to quit. She worked for Spiva, running different art classes and programs for the community. Little Harris had just turned one, and his life was flying by. Meg couldn't shake the feeling she was missing it.

"Can we help in the garden?" Lizzie approached with her younger brother Nick behind her.

"Of course." Meg led them over to the potato bed. She watched them a moment, but they had learned the difference between plants and weeds and didn't need her help. She turned on the hose and watered another part of the garden.

After several hours outside, the kids were hungry again.

Meg slapped together peanut butter and jelly sandwiches. She loaded plastic plates with the sandwiches and SunChips, then set them down on the wood picnic table outside. The children gathered around and ate as if she'd been starving them for a week.

Meg snapped a few pictures of them. Of course the quality on her phone wasn't nearly as good as with a real camera, but at least she had a way to capture these moments whenever she wanted to.

She ate a few chips and checked her watch. Scott had the Weedeater out, and she knew it would be awhile before he finished. "All right, let's go in, guys," she said, ushering the children into the kitchen. "Time to clean up, then quiet time!"

"More chips!" Harris cried, pulling the empty bag out of the trash. The tiny crumbs scattered all over the floor. He plopped himself down in the middle and started eating them.

"Harris! No!" Meg cried. Too late. She shook her head. "All right, little man. Off you go." She swatted his diapered bum and sent him into the living room after his siblings. No big deal. Just a pile of chips, after all. She got the broom out and swept up the mess.

Meg could hear Lizzie playing a board game in the living room and baby Harris babbling to himself. She wandered in to check on Nick and found him conked out on the living room floor on top of a pillow.

"Goodness, Nicks," she said, bending over to smooth his hair. Usually her children needed their own beds to fall asleep. He must really be tired if he could pass out on the floor like that.

Meg straightened and made eye contact with her oldest. "I'm going to start a load of laundry. When I come back, it's naptime. Got it, Lizzie?"

Lizzie nodded, still moving the pieces from Chutes and Ladders all over the board. "Okay."

Chapter Three

Sunday afternoon, May 22, 2011
Approximately 3 Hours Before Tornado Strikes

"It was like something inside me snapped, I felt as if the ground fell away from underneath me and I was free falling." —
Michelle Short

The Borup Household
A single-story chapel
Less than a mile from the path of destruction

As usual, the Borups parked in the east lot. The front of the church faced the high school to the south, but there was no parking there. The large group filed in the east doors. They passed the plaques with the names of all the youth who had earned awards through goal-setting and service.

Melinda had just been at the church the night before, doing the music for the youth dance. Except that time, she'd been on the stage at the other end of the building. Now she sat in front of the congregation, waiting for her turn to lead the music.

The way the chapel was set up always made it seem fuller than it actually was. The divider between the chapel and the gym was open, with rows and rows of chairs set up, just waiting for people to fill them. David sat in a pew in front of her, their herd of children around him and in the pew behind. The Borup family took up two pews, a fact that always made Melinda chuckle.

She closed her eyes and took several deep breaths, trying to let the religious atmosphere calm her after the mad rush to get out the door. The three youngest boys had all gone on strike, refusing to put on shirts and ties. By the time Melinda got them ready and into the car, they were on the verge of being late.

Melinda hated feeling rushed. Sunday was a day of rest, but she didn't feel rested. Her blood pounded in her temples, and she wasn't in the best of moods. She opened her eyes. In spite of their reluctance, all of the children looked groomed and handsome. She exhaled and let her shoulders relax.

The boys sat so reverently, arms folded across their laps, eyes on the speaker. The youngest met her eyes and grinned, and she grinned back. Her frustration melted away. They were just little boys, after all.

"And now we'll sing hymn number two twenty-one."

That was her cue. Melinda stood as the organ started to play. She raised her arm and led the congregation in the spiritual song. Her life revolved around music. Since Richard was still in high school, she spent a lot of time volunteering with the marching band, making her an official "band mom." She had done it for her daughter while she went through school, and it thrilled her that so many of her kids were musically inclined. Her oldest daughter played the cello, Richard the tuba, another daughter the viola, and a son the euphonium. The music washed over her, taking with it the last of her stress.

Halfway through the meeting, Richard's ride to graduation stood to leave. Melinda nodded at him, urging him to leave as well. Though only a sophomore, he was one of the only tuba players in the band, and therefore a sought-after commodity.

Church ended at four, but Melinda found it impossible to gather up her family and get everyone out of the building before four twenty. She found the younger boys right before they joined in a game of chase in the gym. "Out to the car. Now."

They ran out the door before she could chastise them further.

The next task was to find her husband. David was easily the hardest person to get out of the church building; it seemed he had to stop and chat with every person he passed in the hall. Melinda finally found him and stood by his side, a forced smile on her face, until he said goodbye to his conversation partner and followed her outside.

Ten minutes later they piled out of the car at home, everyone complaining about hunger.

"Change clothes!" Melinda said, hanging her church bags on several pegs in the entryway. She and her daughter had spent the previous week in Eureka Springs, Arkansas, having a mother-daughter getaway, and she hadn't had the chance to plan Sunday dinner. She looked at David. "Did you have something in mind for today?"

He shook his head. "Nope."

Which meant everyone was on their own. "I'll put the leftovers on the counter. Everyone can eat what they want." Melinda disappeared into the master bedroom to change out of her church clothes.

The McMinn Family
Amber's house: A single-story white house
Less than a mile from the path of destruction

After several hours of heavy grunt work, Kayla and Justin got Amber's big items moved. Amber looked excited even though her stuff littered the kitchen and living room. Kayla waited in the house with the children while Justin unloaded the last few items.

"It's way past lunch time. Have you eaten?" Amber asked, moving into her kitchen and opening the fridge. "I have a few things in here."

Kayla shook her head. "We haven't eaten since breakfast." Nearly four hours ago now. "I'm hungry, actually. We took food to your mom, but who knows what goes through her head? She wouldn't touch it."

"Good luck with that," Amber said, her brown eyes

wide. "Well, here." She opened the freezer and pulled out burritos and hamburger patties. "Let's get cooking."

Kayla made cereal for the baby. "What time is it?"

Amber checked her phone. "Almost three thirty."

"We should go." Kayla began gathering up the children and their food. "My dad's coming over for dinner."

"Sure." Amber nodded.

Justin stepped into the house and deposited a plastic Walmart bag filled with small knickknacks. He wiped his brow. "All done, Amber."

Kayla handed him the baby, already moving toward the door. "Let's go."

Amber came around the counter and hugged her brother. "Thanks for all your help."

"No problem," he grunted, shifting the baby to the other arm.

They piled into the car. Kayla turned it on and rolled down the windows to vent the hot air while Justin buckled in the kids. She slid over to her side when he opened the door.

"Maybe *we* should move," Kayla said, her voice light as she buckled her seatbelt. "That was a lot of fun."

"Nuh-uh!" Justin exploded, backing out of the driveway. "I never want to lift heavy furniture again! The best thing we can do is just stay put."

Kayla burst out laughing. "Calm down! I was just joking!" She patted Justin's head, lowering her hand to play with the hair at the nape of his neck.

"Not funny," he grumbled, but he leaned his head back so she could reach him better.

They pulled into their driveway and Kayla helped the kids out of their car seats, all the while thinking she'd better get the steaks going; an hour wasn't a lot of time to prepare for dinner.

Steak and potatoes was the traditional Sunday dinner in their house. Baby Clayton began crying in the living room. Hoping her fiancé was taking care of him, Kayla stopped at the fridge and pulled out the steaks.

"Kayla!" Justin yelled. "Can you see what's wrong with the baby?"

She sighed and put the cold meat in the oven. "He's just tired, Justin!" She didn't get a response, but she didn't expect one. Kayla washed her hands and followed the sound of Clayton's crying. Finding him alone in the playroom, she covered him with kisses. "Oh little bug, you're tired, huh?"

He wrapped his chubby arms around her neck and sobbed. Kayla made him a bottle, then carried him to the back of the house and lay him in his crib. She wrapped his favorite blanket around him. "Sleep tight, baby bug." She turned out the light, gently closing the door.

"Clayton's down," she told Justin, who had already seated himself in front of the TV. "I'm heading over to the neighbor's to use the phone."

"'Kay," he responded, not looking up.

Kayla crossed the street to call her dad again, grateful the neighbors never complained about her using their phone.

Her father didn't answer. Since he worked nights as a police officer for the Miami Oklahoma Police Department, he was probably sleeping.

"Hey, it's me," she said to his answering machine. "We'll eat in about an hour, so head on over."

She hung up the phone just as a siren went off.

"What's that?" she murmured. "Tornado siren?" Kayla frowned up at the blue sky and hurried across the street.

The Scaggs Household

After the kids were down for naps, Meg changed into her running shoes.

"Scott," she said, coming into the living room.

He lay spread out on the couch, looking close to sleep himself. A football game played onscreen, the sportscaster's excited voice buzzing like a mosquito. "Yeah?" he said, not lifting his hooded eyes from the TV.

59

Meg sat down next to him. Scott worked hard. Before graduation, his days had lasted from seven a.m. to seven p.m., Monday through Saturday. Today was the first day of many more relaxing ones, she hoped. "I'm going for a jog. See you in about an hour?"

"Sure, no problem."

Meg headed out the door and down the steps. She tried to get a jog in every day, but Sundays were definitely her favorite. This was the day she could leave the kids at home with Scott and run without a stroller to push. She tried to get an extra-long jog in because of this.

Meg jogged around the block, passing the muffler shop on the corner. She didn't know the owner personally, but her dog Ellie always ran along the fence next to his house when she came on runs with Meg, barking playfully at his Husky. Meg waved and he waved back.

Meg ran her usual loop, then jogged through the Campbell Parkway, a large park with a running trail. She ran this circular path several times, getting her exercise without putting more distance between her and the house. She liked it because if she needed to go home for any reason, she was never too far away.

The wind began to pick up, pulling her hair free from its ponytail and whipping her face with it. "Time to go home," Meg said, increasing her speed.

The game still played on the television, but Scott's eyes were closed. He didn't move when she came in. Meg closed the door quietly to the master bedroom, trying not to disturb him.

She showered, then put on a pair of slacks and a button up blouse. One thing she would miss about working was dressing up. She'd have to find other opportunities to put on heels and dangly earrings...like dinner with her dad.

Scott appeared in the mirror behind her. "Did you ever find a sitter for Baby H?"

"No." Meg shook her head and leaned into the mirror, putting on lipstick. To celebrate Scott's graduation, Meg's dad was treating them to dinner at Outback. While Meg didn't mind having her two older children along, she had hoped to leave Harris with a sitter, especially since her mom was out of town. Usually she could count on her to help wrangle the kids.

Scott straightened his tie and shrugged. "Your sister will be there with her five kids?"

"Yeah." Meg met his eyes in the mirror.

"Well, then no one will notice our three."

She laughed. "Yeah, I'm sure you're right."

The Mitchells
Webb City
6 miles from the path of destruction

Though it wasn't quite dinnertime, Nellie and James stopped at Taco Gringo on the way to Webb City.

"Storm coming in," James said, turning off the car.

Nellie looked up at the cloudy sky. "Yeah, I was listening to the same radio station," she teased. Still, the sky didn't look frightening, just a bit overcast. The weather felt warm and comfortable. "We'll be in Cade's basement if anything should happen. It's safe there."

James opened the door and got out.

Nellie followed. "No drive-thru today?"

James shrugged. "Well, you know, I just thought it would be fun to sit outside on the little patio. Just us."

"Like every meal," Nellie cracked. "Just us." She didn't mind, though. The idea was sweet.

Nellie ordered her usual: a cheese burrito with a crispy beef taco. She loved the flour tortilla filled with cheese, green onions, and a special sauce. She considered it a melted, cheesy perfection. A strong breeze blew the sun umbrella above their white table on the patio. Nellie studied the sky. Big puffy clouds had blown in, round on the bottom like giant marshmallows. The whole sky looked like the bottom of a styrofoam egg carton.

"That's weird," she said.

"What?" James took a huge bite of his taco.

Nellie rolled her eyes and gestured. "The sky. Those are scary looking clouds."

"Oh." He didn't look up.

"That's where scary storms come from."

James took another bite and spoke around a mouth full of food. Typical. "School's almost out."

"Oh, yes." Nellie only had about two weeks of school left. "I can hardly wait for summer."

"It will be nice to have you around this time."

"Like you'll even notice," Nellie said. "You'll be working as usual." But she was excited as well. Usually she taught summer school, but this year she had decided to take the full six weeks off.

James stood up. "You ready? We better get going. It does look like rain in those clouds." He wrinkled a white napkin in his hands.

"Yeah, let's go."

The Divine Household
Piper's mother's house: A multi-level apartment complex
Less than a mile from the path of destruction

Piper's mom called almost as soon as Piper pulled out of Cheddar's parking lot.

"Hi, honey," she said. "Could you come over?"

Her mom had just filed for divorce and moved into her own place. Her emotions were up and down lately, and Piper knew she needed the support. Her mom was her best friend, and the two women spent time together almost every day. She glanced at the clock on the dash. Piper had plenty of time until she needed to pick up her son in Oklahoma. "Sure. I'll be right there."

Piper let herself in the front door. "What's up, Mom?"

"In here," her mom called from the bedroom. "Just folding laundry."

Piper followed the voice and bounced onto the bed next to her mom. "It's just you, Mom. How can you have so much to wash?"

Her mom shrugged. "I don't know…just happens!"

The doorbell rang, and Piper scooted off the bedspread. "Who are you expecting?"

"No one."

The two women walked to the front of the house. Piper watched her mom open the door with a slight look of suspicion, which melted away immediately when she saw her best friend on the step.

"Sheila! Come in!"

"I hope you don't mind that I came by unannounced." Sheila, a large woman, nodded her head at a toddler on her hip. "I have Adam today. Thought we'd come by." She spotted Piper and grinned. "Hi, Piper! Didn't know you were here!"

"Hi." Piper took Adam from Sheila. "I always try to plan my visits around little Adam." She smiled at the blue-eyed boy, earning a shy grin in return.

The Jason Residence

Penny's cell phone rang a little after 3:00 p.m. Absorbed in her book, Penny tried to ignore it. But when it started up again, Pierre looked right at her.

"Don't you hear your phone?

Penny sighed and put her Kindle down. "Yes, of course I hear it," she said, trying to keep the annoyance from her voice. He'd only gotten the cable working again an hour ago, so of course he was a bit edgy.

The phone stopped, but before Penny could relax, it started up again. Penny grabbed a handful of chips from the bowl and made her way to the bedroom. Who would be so insistent to call three times in a row? She glanced at the phone screen.

"Why, hello, Aunt Lucy," Penny said, answering the

63

call. She should've known. The older woman lived alone in her spacious Vegas house, and she and Penny frequently talked for hours. "How are you, dear?"

"Well, I'm doing good, Penny. But I saw on the weather station that you're expecting bad weather in your area. Are you okay?"

Penny pulled back the curtains and peered outside. Sure enough, the wind had picked up, but the sky wasn't even dark. "Oh, don't worry about us, Aunt Lucy. I've lived here all my life. We go through this all the time. It might get bad around Joplin, but nothing bad ever happens here."

Aunt Lucy took a deep breath. "I feel a bit better, then. Just be careful. How's your mama?"

"She's doing well, thank the Lord," Penny said, glad to have a listening ear about her ailing mother. "I just spent the day with her yesterday." The conversation launched into a replay of her mother's recent health ailments as Penny chatted amiably with her aunt.

Cara Edens' Home

Cara's dad showed up at two o'clock. By this time, Cara had succumbed to the heat and opened every window and the front door, in addition to the patio door. Warm sunshine beat down on the concrete outside.

"Knock knock," Mr. Edens said, tapping on the doorframe.

"Come in," Cara replied. She looked up from the couch where she fanned her face with her hand. "I thought you'd be here earlier."

"I mowed your grandparents' lawn. The grass was getting long."

"Well." She stood up. "My AC's out and I'm dying. Can you fix it?"

"Let's take a look."

After a few unsuccessful tries, Mr. Edens shook his head. "Sorry, Cara. Looks like it needs to be charged up. Is this the first time you've tried it all spring?"

She stared back at him, biting back a snippy response. "Yeah, well, it's the first hot day, isn't it?"

"Sure is." He wiped his brow and gathered up the Pack 'n Play. "It's your sister's first day of work."

"Yeah, I know." That's why he needed the Pack 'n Play, after all. "She liking it so far?"

"Don't know yet. We'll hear all about it tonight. I'm fixing a big dinner. Why don't you and Stephen come over and we can all eat together?"

It was a nice idea, and Cara considered the invitation for a moment. She adored her nephew, and her dad was a great cook. She and Stephen often spent Sunday dinner with her family. "Love to, Dad, but I'm finally just relaxing, now that finals are done." She gave a dramatic sigh and leaned against the doorway. "Lots to do with getting ready for summer term, too." That was definitely true. "And Stephen will be really tired when he gets home from work."

"Enough said." Her father smiled, the corners of his eyes crinkling upward. "Thanks for the Pack 'n Play. Anything else you need?"

"No." Cara pushed off the doorway. "We'll see you later."

Chapter Four

Sunday evening, May 22, 2011
Approximately 40 Minutes before Tornado Strikes

*"The wall of black behind the neighbor's house was so foreign,
I had never seen the sky like that, not even at night." – Name
Withheld*

Cara Edens' Home

Cara lay on the couch watching another relaxing movie on Lifetime TV. Stephen would get off work soon. Outside the sun still beat on the apartment, and she wished a breeze would come in and stir up the humid air. Wind blew the trees around, but none of it entered the small building.

A small icon appeared in the right-hand corner of the television screen, flashing a severe Thunderstorm Warning. Cara frowned and leaned forward. That was odd. Usually her father called her to let her know about any weather situations.

The warning said to stay indoors. She glanced again outside at the bright sunshine. Definitely weird.

Cara switched to KOAM, the local news station. Since the only thing the station usually showed was sports, Cara didn't generally watch it. Sure enough, it also showed a Severe Thunderstorm Warning. Cara dialed her dad's phone.

"Hello?" Cara's mom answered.

"Hi, Mom," Cara said, settling back against the couch cushions. "Are we expecting some bad weather?"

"Oh, I think so," Mrs. Edens said. "Your dad's in the shower. He's trying to beat the storm. I think he plans to call you when he gets out."

That sounded like her dad. "Okay," Cara said. Outside thunder rolled, the low sound filling the air. Cara kept waiting for it to break, but it only diminished in sound before starting up again. She listened to it a few minutes, not really hearing what her mom was saying in the background.

The television emitted several high-pitched beeps, and Cara turned her attention back to the screen. "Wait, Mom. Now it says it's a Tornado Warning."

"Really? Turn the news on."

Cara switched channels in time for the announcer, Doug Heady, to say, "We have a possible tornado right over Joplin."

"Mom, he said a tornado," Cara said, her heart starting to pound. She thought of Stephen, on the road somewhere. "What's going on? What do I do?" There was no safe place in her third story apartment. "Do I need to go somewhere?"

"Stay where you are." Cara could hear her mom opening and closing doors. "I'm getting your father out of the shower. We'll call you."

The phone disconnected and Cara stared at the TV, not sure what else to do.

The McMinn Family
A single-story house with blue siding
Less than a mile from the path of destruction

Rain fell lightly while Kayla walked back home. She closed the front door behind her. "Justin!" she called. "Did you hear that siren?"

"What siren?" he yelled back.

Kayla sighed and went into the living room. "*That* siren. The one I hear right now."

"I don't know." He got up, tossing the remote on the coffee table. "I need a smoke."

"Yeah, me too." Justin didn't seem too concerned about

the sirens, so Kayla decided not to worry either. She turned the oven off just in case, then picked up her pack of cigarettes and followed Justin outside.

The alarm stopped going off. Kayla smoked a couple of cigarettes with Justin.

"Did you guys hear about the tornado?"

She turned around as their neighbor Brandon wheeled himself over in his electric wheelchair.

"No, what tornado?" Justin asked. He straightened up, putting out his cigarette.

"A tornado touched down in Carl Junction just a few minutes ago."

"That's pretty close," Justin said.

Too close, Kayla thought. "Let's move the kids into the bathtub. Put a mattress in there, too."

Justin frowned. "I hate to wake Clayton for a false alarm. Are you sure?"

"Yeah."

She went inside and pulled the steaks out of the oven. Looked like dinner would have to wait. She picked up the baby and carried him, still sleeping, to the bathtub. Hopefully he would stay asleep. She put him in his bouncer and set him inside the tub.

"Clark, honey," she called to her oldest, "we're going to sit in the bathtub for a while."

He obliged her, climbing inside. "Why?"

Kayla gave him his blanket, bean bag, and Scooby Doo book. She tucked the baby's blanket around him, the special one his grandma had made for him. "There's a bad storm outside and we're going to wait in here for it to pass. Will you watch your brother?"

Clark's eyes followed her as she stood up. "Where are you going, Mommy?"

"Outside to watch for the storm." She ran her fingers through his hair. "Take care of your brother, okay?" She nudged the book closer to Clark. "Here's your Scooby Doo book. Read to him if he wakes up, okay?"

"Okay."

Kayla first went to Clayton's room and got the mattress from his toddler bed. Just in case, she put it in the bathroom next to the tub. She rejoined Justin in the living room, where he was flipping through channels.

"Anything?" she asked.

He shrugged. "Can't find anything about a tornado. I'm gonna check outside again."

Kayla followed him. Brandon was still outside, and he and Justin struck up a conversation. She pulled out another cigarette. "Well? Any more news?"

Brandon looked up at the blue sky. "Nothing so far."

Just the same light rain as before. Kayla turned to Justin. "Should I put the mattress on top of the kids?"

He shook his head. "I don't think there's any danger. You can probably take the kids out."

Kayla went back inside. She stopped in the kitchen and turned the oven back on, then shoved the steaks inside. Everything would be late now.

Clark looked up at her when she came into the bathroom, and Kayla gave him a big smile. "All right, guys, come on out. Storm's over."

The Borup Household
A two-story, wood-frame house with a basement
1.5 miles from the path of destruction

Melinda's house sat in south Joplin on the line between Shoal Creek and Joplin, about a half mile from I-44. It was the opposite side of town of where the graduation was taking place. Graduation would be over in about thirty minutes. Since the drive would be at least twenty, she wanted to give herself plenty of time. She came out of her room, slipping on a pair of shoes. "Kids! Food's on the counter!"

The thunderous noise of a dozen feet shook the house as the children ran to the kitchen. "You serve everyone,"

Melinda said, giving the serving utensils to David. "There's juice and milk in the fridge. I have to go."

"Why don't you send one of the older two?" David asked, pulling out his chair and sitting down.

Melinda looked at the older children. The two oldest both had their driver's license and could pick up their brother. They were incredibly responsible teens, and definitely capable.

"Then you can stay and eat with us," David pressed.

Melinda shook her head. She remembered something about a thunderstorm coming in that afternoon, and already the wind outside was picking up. "Tempting. But I'll just go this time. There will be a lot of traffic. I'd rather do it." Melinda kissed David's cheek and hurried out the door.

She parked her Honda Pilot opposite the graduation gymnasium and waited for Richard. It felt like she was going the wrong direction, but she wanted to be in the back of the building so he wouldn't have to haul his tuba so far. People streamed out in all directions, and she knew it would be easier for her to spot him than for him to spot her.

It started to sprinkle, and Melinda could see black clouds forming to the west. She stayed in the car, not wanting to get wet. Finally she saw Richard, his broad shoulders and height making him easier to spot. Melinda stood up out of the car and waved. "Richard!"

He'd already seen her. He pushed his way through the crowd, hefting his tuba in both hands. "Hey Mom."

"Hey, honey. How did it go?"

"Great."

Melinda's phone beeped, and she pulled it out of her purse to check the text. It was from Weather.com. "Oh my mercy. A tornado touched down in Baxter Springs. It says it's coming this way."

"This way?" Richard asked, lifting an eyebrow.

Melinda didn't get the chance to answer before the tornado sirens went off. "Actually, it's going past our

70

house. Hurry."

She popped the trunk and helped him fit the large instrument inside. Anxiety made her clumsy, and she kept dropping her phone. She texted her daughter and told her to take the kids into the safe room. She felt a wave of gratitude for David's foresight. He'd insisted on having a concrete room added to the house. It was built into the hillside, and it was the safest room in the house.

Richard slammed the trunk just as the tornado siren stopped. "Got it."

Was it over? Melinda's shoulders relaxed. "All right, let's get out of here."

Heavy traffic impeded their exit, as every person who had been at graduation finagled their car into position to leave.

The Scaggs Household

Meg finished dressing the kids and started herding them out to the car. She stopped her three-year-old, Nick.

"Nick. Where are your shoes?" She ushered him back to his room and began the desperate hunt for matching shoes. "Scott! Make sure all the kids have shoes on!"

A few minutes later, she added Nick to the line of kids getting into car seats and boosters. The wind had picked up, and it blew her jangly earrings around like wind chimes.

She hopped into the car next to Scott and slammed the door shut, pulling against the wind. "Do Lizzie and Harris have shoes on?" They might live in Missouri, but the hillbilly jokes stopped there.

"Yep. No barefoot kids."

"Good." Meg nodded. "Wow, is there a storm coming, or what?" She glanced down at her own feet. She wore black flats instead of her usual heels, and it made her feel dressed down. Did she have time to run in and change them? She brushed it off. No, they were already running late.

"No idea." Scott put the car in reverse and looked over

71

his shoulder. "Maybe call your dad, let him know we're coming."

Meg heard the sirens as they backed down the driveway. "What is that?"

"Tornado sirens?"

"Tornado!" Meg glanced back at the three children in their car seats and swiveled back to look out the window. "Never mind, forget about Outback. Everyone into the basement!"

For a moment Meg remained in her chair, hand poised over the seatbelt button while she stared at the sky. Something about the dark swirling mass of clouds disturbed her. It felt very, very, very still, even while the clouds looked like a pot of boiling water ready to simmer over.

The Mitchells

Nellie and James were a block away from Cade's house when the first tornado siren went off.

"Good thing we're going into the basement." Nellie shot James a grin as she slammed the car door behind her.

Cade walked over to the car when they pulled up and joined them at the curb. "Guess they're predicting a big storm coming this way."

"Yeah." James ran a hand over his thick, curly hair, covering up the gray on the sides. "Which way do you think it will go?"

Cade shrugged. "No idea. Guess it'll come from Carl Junction and keep heading into Joplin. It may or may not hit us here."

Nellie shifted her feet, impatient to get into the darkroom. "But we'll be safe. It's not like it could take out the whole house."

"Right." Cade turned around and led them back inside. He grabbed a radio and took it down to the basement.

Nellie got to work setting up her negatives while Cade

and James chatted. The radio station gave several different predictions about where the storm was heading. Nellie didn't worry too much at first, as it said there was a tornado in Alba. Then it started heading down 171, which would be right in their direction. A set of three beeps went off, indicating the emergency broadcast system.

"Tornado Warning for Joplin," the newscaster said.

Nellie dipped one negative in the solution, letting it sit for a minute. "Do you think one will actually hit this time?"

"Not likely." James settled back in his chair. "They never do."

Nellie's cell phone dinged, and she picked it up to read the text message.

"Stay safe," her friend Morgan said.

Nellie laughed. She got the reference to the inside joke they shared. Her thumbs moved rapidly over the keypad, texting out a response. "Right. Better go to Walmart and stock up."

"Got my safety gear," came Morgan's response.

The Jason Residence

"Cable's out again," Pierre said, distracting Penny from her phone conversation with Aunt Lucy. He got up to mess with it and Penny's call-waiting beeped.

"Hold on, Aunt Lucy, it's my daughter." Penny clicked over. Pierre's youngest daughter lived with them, but today she was out with her mother. "Hey, sweetie, how are you?"

"Penny? I'm at the Fashion Bug with my mom."

Penny knew the store. It was located with most of the shopping centers, on the west side of Joplin. "Are you having a nice time?"

"The sirens are going off, Penny. We're going to go home, but I wanted to tell you where I am first." An edge of nervousness riddled her stepdaughter's voice.

Pierre still hadn't gotten the cable back on. Penny glanced out the window again. The sky was darker, but nothing threatening appeared on the horizon. "No, dear, don't leave. Just stay where you are until the siren stops. It's better not to be on the road if it gets bad."

"Okay. I'll tell my mom."

The call disconnected. "Aunt Lucy? Still there?"

Pierre interrupted her. "Penny, I'm concerned. It doesn't look good out there."

Penny couldn't help rolling her eyes. Even Pierre was nervous? Covering the phone so her aunt wouldn't get worked up again, Penny hissed, "Pierre, nothing ever happens here. We're fine."

"It's solid black outside."

Penny ignored him. She'd just checked, and it wasn't that dark. She settled back on the sofa, letting her aunt carry the conversation for now.

The Divine Household

Storm clouds gathered in the sky out the window. Piper put down the blocks she was playing with and gathered up her purse.

"Mom, I'm heading out." She shouldered her purse and blew a kiss at Adam. "Time to pick up Michael."

"Already?" Her mom checked her watch as if that would change the time. "You don't need to be there until six o'clock."

"I know." Piper had already done the math. "But I want to go home and then go to the interstate. Plus it looks like it's going to rain. So I'll just go now."

Her mom shrugged as if Piper's logic didn't make much sense to her. "All right. Call me when you get back."

"Of course."

Piper took her usual route, following Maiden Lane to Schifferdecker. It was normally only a half hour drive, but she wasn't sure what traffic would be like at this time of day. Bad weather could slow her down, too. She turned on the XM radio and sang along, letting the miles fly by under her car tires.

Chapter Five

Sunday at 5:40 pm, May 22, 2011
Approximately 3 Minutes before Tornado Impact

*"The noise was so oppressive that it was hard to imagine any
other alternative than death."* — Morgan Meyer

Cara Edens' Home

Cara leaped from the couch when the tornado sirens
went off. *It must be close,* she thought, her heart hammering.
She flipped her phone open and stared at the unanswered
calls to her father and boyfriend. Where was Stephen? He
hadn't answered any of the four calls. He should be on his
way home from Walmart now. Cara knew he didn't like to
talk and drive at the same time, but still...this was kind of
important.

The shrill warning on the TV rang out again and then
the picture flashed to a bright blue screen as the signal
disappeared. Cara tried changing the channel and messing
with the cables, but nothing came back on. She sat down
again on the couch, staring at the blank television. Would
she hear the tornado before it got to her house? Was there
something she should do?

The balcony door was still open. Cara craned her neck
and gazed outside, unwilling to move from the couch.
The sky had darkened to nearly pitch black in the past
ten minutes. Her wish for a breeze had been granted; the
trees swung back and forth like little slingshots. It didn't
seem possible that the wind could move the thick trunks
that much. It blew through the apartment, brushing her
hair back from her face. Rain slapped against the wooden

railing, mingling with the louder ping of hail.

The front door banged open and Cara shot to her feet. Stephen stood in the entryway, rain pooling on the linoleum floor.

"Yikes," he said, his eyes dark beneath his furrowed brow. "It's hailing out there."

"Thank goodness you're home," Cara said, resisting the urge to throw herself into his arms. One hand crept toward her teeth and she forced it down before she bit her nails. She'd kicked that nasty habit years ago. "The tornado sirens have been going off for almost ten minutes." She checked her phone again. Why hadn't her dad called back yet? He liked to stay off the phone during electrical storms, just to be safe, but didn't he know this was an emergency?

Stephen nodded. "You could tell there was some kinda storm in the air. I knew I was driving toward it. The sky was all black. Kind of scary, with the sirens going off and all."

The lights flickered one second before the house plunged into darkness. Cara lurched to the kitchen cabinets, where she kept a flashlight. "What's going on? Could you see a tornado?" Surely not. They never got tornadoes around here, just bad thunderstorms and Tornado Warnings. The sirens went off several times every spring, and the only action she'd ever taken was to watch the clouds. Then again, she'd never seen a storm like this, either. The flashlight's narrow beam guided her back to the balcony. She walked outside, cracking her knuckles.

The McMinn Family

Kayla carried baby Clayton into the living room in his bouncer. Justin lounged on the couch with the TV on. Clayton immediately began reaching for toys, letting his chair rock him. Kayla fluffed up the pillows before getting comfortable next to Justin.

Tree branches dancing next to the window caught her

eye. Kayla stood and pulled the blinds up. In the few minutes since she'd come inside, the sky had darkened. A heavy wind blew the trees back and forth, reminding her of scenes she'd seen in movies, of palm trees during hurricanes. The tree in front of the house bent so hard in the wind that it almost touched the ground. "It looks pretty bad out there, babe."

"Yeah?" Her fiancé stood and turned on the radio, scanning the stations.

A high-pitched sound rose on the waves of the wind, so faint she hardly heard it. As it rose in volume and descended again, Kayla realized it was the tornado siren again.

She turned around, already hurrying back to the couch. "Justin!" she cried, wrapping an arm around Clark and pulling the baby from his bouncer. "It's coming!"

She saw Justin go to the back door, but Kayla didn't stop. Adrenaline pumped through her, and she knew she didn't have much time. Carrying the children like footballs, she charged into the bathroom.

Both children cried as Kayla put them in the tub. "Shh. It's okay. Mommy's here." Kayla patted their faces and climbed inside. She wrapped her arms around them, using her body as one more shield. She could feel her pulse racing in her neck, and she swallowed a lump in her throat.

"What's a tornado sound like?" Justin called from the living room.

Kayla forgot sometimes that he wasn't from around here. He'd grown up in Denver. "Like a train!" she shouted back.

Justin appeared in the doorway and hurdled into the bathtub so fast that Kayla did a double take.

"I heard it!" he yelled, even as the noise outside drowned out his words.

"The mattress!" Kayla pulled the children closer and hunkered down in the bottom of the tub. "Pull it on top of us!"

Justin grabbed the mattress and huddled down in the

tub, holding the mattress over them.

"You didn't close the door!" Kayla shouted over the roar that filled the house. It sounded like thunder that didn't stop. The bathtub began to shake like the ground next to a railroad track when a train rolls by.

Justin started to move, but she grabbed his arm. "No time! Just leave it open!"

The Divine Household
Gas station in Afton, Oklahoma
40 miles from the path of destruction

Piper came up on the Afton exit almost half an hour earlier than she needed to be there. She pulled into the appointed Chevron and decided to check Facebook. She started scrolling through updates.

One status caught her eye. "Holy cow, I'm looking right at a funnel cloud coming at me."

Her heart surged. What? Had a tornado gone into Joplin? She turned off her XM radio and flipped to a local channel.

"…tornado is on the ground in Joplin. Repeat, a tornado is on the ground in Joplin. Take cover now."

She flipped to another one. "...has been spotted. The tornado is currently in the south but moving quickly. Please seek shelter immediately."

Every station was the same. Piper sucked in a deep breath, waves of hot panic washing over her. Her hand trembled as she hit the speed dial on her phone to call her mom.

"Hello?"

"Mom," Piper said, the words not leaving her mouth fast enough, "there's a tornado on the south side of town. You need to take cover."

"Hang on." Piper heard wind blowing loudly in the background. "I'm looking out the door. I don't see anything."

"Take cover!" Piper yelled.

TORNADO WARNING
Melinda and Richard Borup
A Honda Pilot
Less than a mile from the path of destruction

Melinda turned left on Dusquene, heading toward 7th Street. Richard stopped staring out the window to look at her.

"Mom. Aren't we going home?"

She nodded. "Yes." Most definitely.

"But you didn't take two-forty-nine."

Melinda paused a moment before nodding again. "Yes, I know." She had no idea why she'd decided not to take the highway. It was the fastest way home. But the thought of going that way made her more nervous than she already was, and she was too jittery to fight the feeling. She gnashed her front teeth together.

Richard shrugged and went back to studying the sky. "Whatever." He pressed buttons on Melinda's iPod and turned on the Mormon Tabernacle Choir.

As the music spilled out of the car speakers, Melinda relaxed. The storm was behind them now. She turned down 7th, then Main Street.

"Mom," Richard said, his voice tense. "Look." He pointed to the west.

Melinda risked a glance and gasped. A thick black wall of cloud moved toward them. She pushed on the gas, not caring about safe speeds right now. "I just want to get home. I just want to get home, Richard."

"Okay, Mom." His knuckles turned white where he gripped the door handle, eyes still on the moving wall. "Just get home."

Melinda drove the car over a hill and turned onto 32nd Street. The hairs on the back of her neck stood on end, and hail and rain started pelting the car. It came down so hard and fast that the windshield wipers couldn't make a dent in it. The car began to swerve left and right on the road.

Melinda screamed. "Richard! I can't control it!"

He reached over and grabbed the steering wheel, trying to help hold the car on course.

"Where's our street? Where's our turn?" Melinda cried, a desperate, panicked feeling flooding her chest.

Richard squinted through the window. "There it is, Mom! There!"

Melinda accelerated only to find it wasn't a street at all, but a patch of grass. The car lurched to a stop. "I can't see!" She recognized the hill in front of them. St. John's hospital was just on the other side. "I'm sorry! I couldn't find the street!"

"Just put the emergency brake on, Mom!"

What good is that going to do? Melinda thought. Still, she put it on.

"Mom." Richard grabbed her hand. His sweaty palms slipped on her fingers. "We need to say a prayer right now."

"Yes." Melinda closed her eyes. "Please, Heavenly Father, protect us. Protect our families. Please watch over us."

The Scaggs Household

Scott opened the car door just as it started raining. Hail fell, big enough to dent the car.

Meg grabbed his arm. "Park in the garage," she said. She was glad she'd spent several hours yesterday cleaning it out.

Scott hit the garage door opener and slid the car inside. He closed the door while Meg ushered the children into the house. She turned the TV on to the local news channel as she walked past it. "Take the kids downstairs to play, okay, Lizzie?" Both the playroom and Harris's room were in the bottom level. The laundry room was also down there. The wall in Harris's room sat next to dirt, and was probably the safest room in the house.

"All right," Lizzie said.

The hail increased in size, pelting the house. Meg stayed

upstairs, keeping one eye on the TV and the other on the weather outside. Her heart pounded in her throat. At least the kids were in the safest part of the house, if something should happen. Meg didn't want to appear paranoid or jumpy. It was just a Tornado Warning, after all. She couldn't even count how many times in her life she had gone downstairs to sit out a warning. This was just part of springtime.

But this storm scared her.

It's no big deal, she told herself. *This is normal. In a moment the warning will pass, and we'll all get back in the car and go out to dinner.*

The Tornado Warning flashed big on the TV screen, but that wasn't what caught Meg's attention. She leaned in closer as the anchorman narrated the huge wall of cloud the camera picked up behind him. The wall hit the transformer tower, sending flashes of light throughout the cloud mass. The anchorman's voice became emotional.

"It does look like there is a tornado on the ground in the southern portions of Joplin, just to the south of our station here. It is taking out those power lines, you can see those flashes on there. Everybody, take cover. I am telling you to take cover right now! We do have a tornado on the ground."

Meg jumped to her feet. This was real, and it was happening now. "Scott! Get in the basement right now!" Thunder crashed outside, and the power went out in the house. Meg dashed through the kitchen and grabbed the hand-operated radio. She needed to track this storm.

She pounded down the stairs and found all the kids in the playroom. Meg opened her mouth to say something when a window blew out behind them. Lizzie screamed, and Meg flinched before grabbing her daughter. "Come on, guys. Into the laundry room." Meg grabbed the baby with the other arm and shoved her son in front of them. "Scott!"

"I'm here." He hurdled the stairs and shoved the laundry

room door open. Across his shoulder he had Meg's purse, and in his arms, the dog.

Meg handed Baby Harris to him. She and the other two children smashed into the space against the wall next to the washer and dryer.

The Mitchells

Nellie had managed to develop one photo when the newscaster interrupted with the Emergency Broadcast System.

"A tornado is on the ground in Joplin on Seventh Street and Range Line. Take cover immediately."

Nellie froze. "No way. There is not a tornado at Seventh and Range Line!" It couldn't be. They lived half a mile south of there. Faces of coworkers and friends flashed through her mind. She had lived in Joplin for the past six years and it was home. Her husband, James, had grown up in Joplin, and all of his family still lived there.

The radio announcer was going over the standard procedure for Tornado Warnings. "If you have no underground shelter, get to an interior room with no windows."

Nellie yanked out her phone and started texting her friends. "R u OK? Pls respond." She texted Morgan and Jason, two of their good friends. Then she texted her neighbor to see if her and James's house was okay. She sent off a few more to family and friends. "What's happening? Where R U? Is everything OK?"

She stared at her phone for a full minute, waiting anxiously for some response, but nothing came. Cold shivers ran down her spine.

The Jason Residence

Pierre took the phone from Penny, his face tight, and hung up on Aunt Lucy.

"What's wrong?" Penny asked, alarmed at his frenzied expression.

"We need to get in the basement. Right now."

A prickle of fear entered her heart. What was he so concerned about? She crossed the room and opened the front door. The wind blew hard, bending the trees in the front nearly to the ground. Rain pounded around them. The sky had turned a blackish-gray color. *I'm sure it's nothing,* she told herself, gnawing her lower lip. *Just another thunderstorm.*

"Close the door," Pierre said, grabbing her arm.

"I think you're supposed to leave it open," Penny said. Wasn't that the theory? Let the wind blow through the open doors?

Pierre slammed it shut. "Let's get downstairs."

"I'm coming," she said, trying to shake him loose.

Pierre didn't let go. He had his laptop under one arm and guided Penny to the windowless half-bath under the stairs. The house trembled and the wind howled around them. Pierre grabbed Penny's hand. He breathed hard, sweat beading on his face, and Penny's heart began to beat faster.

"Oh! Bella!" she cried. "We left the dog upstairs!"

Pierre squeezed her hand and rested the laptop across his thigh. "No time, Pen. She'll be fine. It's all going to be okay."

Penny's free hand ached, and she looked down to see her cell phone clutched tightly in a fist. She thought about calling her aunt back, letting her know what was happening. Glass shattered somewhere outside the bathroom, and she jerked her head around. "What was that?" The bathroom door was ajar, and Penny pressed an eye to the crack. "The windows, Pierre!" She gasped in shock at the sight of the shattered glass on the basement floor. "The wind blew out the windows!"

"Close that door!" Pierre put the laptop on the ground and pushed on the door. The wind pushed back so hard that he couldn't get it to latch. Over his shoulder, Penny spotted Bella racing toward them.

"Bella! Bella's coming!"

Pierre stopped his efforts for a moment and reached out to help the dog into the tiny room. The wind howled around them, shaking the exposed timbers under the stairway. "Penny, help!" Pierre yelled. "I can't get her!"

Bella whined in his arms, and Penny grabbed onto a leg just as the wind yanked the dog away from them. Bella howled in fear as the storm sucked her out a blown-out window.

"Bella!" Penny cried, unable to wrap her mind around what she'd just seen. Her hands began to shake, and she pulled on the door. "Pierre! She's gone! Oh Lord, this is the end!"

Chapter Six

"I felt like a frenzied animal trying to protect her young. I would have clawed my way through any amount of debris with my bare hands to get to my children if need be." — Michelle Short

The Scaggs Household

Meg pulled out her phone and texted her sister. "Left playroom. Windows blowing out."

She could hear more glass shattering throughout the house. She hoped that would be the extent of the damage.

A noise like a roaring waterfall sounded just outside the laundry room door. The door rattled, threatening to come off its hinges. The kids started screaming and Meg threw herself on top of them.

"Mom!" Lizzie shouted. Her small hands pushed on Meg's shoulders. "Get off!"

Scott gripped the door, still holding little Harris and Ellie in one arm, his biceps bulging with the effort to hold on. The baby screamed and clung to the dog. The walls trembled and Meg clutched her other children to her. *I need to get Harris from Scott*, she thought, but she couldn't let go of Lizzie and Nick. The wind had grown fingers, and it wormed its way through any crack or crevice in the walls.

The door bowed where Scott held it closed, and Meg felt the air being sucked from the room. Nick screamed and squeezed her arm. Meg imagined he could also feel the wind, pulling at him. Her heart pounded in her ears, almost drowning out the sound.

The whole house was going to go, and she and her family would go with it. Meg couldn't do anything except watch it happen.

The Divine Household

It killed Piper to be so far away from her mom in this moment of crisis, to be unable to physically make sure she did what she needed to do.

"Calm down, Piper," her mom said. The background noises stopped. "I'm in the bathroom now."

"All right," Piper breathed. "Just stay there."

She hung up the phone and turned the volume up on the radio.

"I'm on Range Line," the newscaster was saying. "This place is gone. This place is gone."

Piper couldn't focus on the rest of his words. Her hands clenched the steering wheel. Gone. The shopping mall. Home Depot. Hobby Lobby. Walmart.

Piper's ex-husband showed up a few minutes early with her son. She hopped out of the car, anxious to turn around and go home. The rain came down in sheets, and the wind blew her short brown hair around her face. "Did you hear about the tornado?" she shouted.

"Tornado?" He looked around at the sky.

"Not here. In Joplin."

Her ex focused on her. "No. What happened?"

"I don't really know yet." Piper placed a hand on her son's shoulder. "We better go. Tell Daddy bye." She hurried him into the car, closing the door and jumping in before they could get too soaked. Then she drove the car back onto I-44.

The McMinn Family

"Maybe it won't hit us," Kayla said, clutching Justin

with a desperate hope.

"No, I saw it," Justin said, raising his voice to match the noise. "It's huge and coming right at us."

She heard crashing and shattering sounds from the kitchen. She winced. "Oh, Justin! There goes the kitchen!" She hated to lose her flat-top stove, the wood cabinets.

Something hit the ground with a thud, followed by the sound of breaking glass. Justin gritted his teeth. "No, that was my TV going into the fish tank."

Kayla gasped, picturing the 55" plasma TV colliding with the 150-gallon fish tank. She imagined all those fish flailing about on broken shards of glass, including the 8-inch long ten-year-old Oscar fish. She shook the image from her head.

Justin peered out of the bathtub through the crook in his arm. His forearms trembled with fatigue from holding down the mattress. "I can see things flying around out there."

The bathtub trembled, then moved and lifted up.

Kayla screamed. "Oh God, save us!"

The children whimpered, and Kayla tightened her grip on them. The bathtub tilted and they all rolled to one side. Justin yelled, his muscles clenching as he struggled to keep the mattress on top of them.

It felt like a bulldozer rammed into the bathtub, shoving it into the laundry room. The house shifted and something hit the mattress with a dull thud. Justin yelped. Darkness filled the area in the bathtub. Clayton's little cries echoed in their porcelain cave.

"What was that?" Kayla cried.

"A wall fell on us." Justin's voice came from the blackness. "I'm okay. Something hit my head pretty hard, but I'm okay."

The noise and shaking went on forever.

The baby still cried. Kayla tried to comfort him, caressing his tiny body. "Oh!" she said. "His leg is pinned by the wall!" Somehow he'd gotten his leg out of the bathtub, and the wall held it to the rim. She tugged on his leg, successfully freeing him.

And then everything stopped. Kayla found her whole body trembling, and tears leaked from her eyes.

The silence was deafening after all the noise. Seconds passed, and her heart thundered in her ears. "Is it over?" she gasped.

"Help! Help us!" Sobs and screaming began to take the place of the storm.

"Help me!" The voice drifted through the mattress, muffled and indistinct. But Kayla recognized it as that of their wheelchair-bound neighbor, Brandon.

Justin moved, shoving the wall off the mattress. "I've got to go help him."

"No!" Kayla sat up as the mattress moved away and clutched at his hand. "What if it comes back?" She stared at the flattened house around them. Ambulance lights flickered in the distance.

"Can't stay here," he replied. "There's no place to hide anymore. We'll all die."

Justin climbed out, but Kayla didn't move. She huddled next to the children, holding them close.

Another neighbor, Carla, stumbled by, holding her small daughter by the hand. "My baby!" she screamed. "I can't find my baby!"

"What happened, Carla? Where's your husband?" Kayla couldn't bring herself to move. Fear paralyzed her.

"I was holding the baby!" Carla sobbed. "The wind ripped him right out of my arms! The house is gone and I can't find him anywhere!"

Even from in the bathtub, Kayla had felt the wind trying to pry her children from her grip. "Oh Carla! Where's Joe?"

"He went to the store. He's not here." Carla's shoulders shook. "Help me! Please!"

"I'll help you, Carla." Justin took her daughter and put her in the tub with Kayla and the boys. He covered up their half of the bathtub with the mattress again. Rain poured in on them from the roofless house.

"Try to stay dry," Justin said.

Clark cried, and Kayla scooted back under the mattress, her arms wrapped around the two boys and Carla's daughter. With the mattress over the top of them, she couldn't really see anything. It was pitch black, and Kayla worried that might be frightening the children more. Yet she couldn't bring herself to move the mattress. She felt safer beneath it. Kayla lifted one edge of it and peeked out. All the walls in the house were gone, and nothing impeded her view to the street. Or beyond it, for that matter. Most of the walls on the entire block were gone.

A cold chill flooded Kayla's body. It looked like a war zone out there. Where on earth was her father? Kayla dropped the mattress back down and hunkered around her children. The baby kept crying, putting his fingers in his mouth and sobbing. Little Clark didn't hardly move. He wrapped his arms around his knees and stared at the bathtub wall, not making a sound. Kayla worried he was in shock.

Carla came back, sobbing. "Kayla, give me my girl."

Kayla handed back the little girl. "Did you find him?"

"No. We can't find him. I see light down the street. I'm going to get help. Pray for us."

"I will," Kayla said, trying not to cry herself. She hugged Clark and Clayton, so grateful her little boys hadn't been taken.

"Kayla?" Justin lifted the side of the mattress and knelt next to them. "It's bad, Kayla. Across the street—" he broke off and shook his head. "A light pole fell on the house. It crushed the kids. I helped lift it off, but..." he shook his head again. "We couldn't save one of the little boys. I can't find Stephanie or her family, either. Their house is gone. I'm starting to worry."

"Oh no," Kayla whispered. Stephanie was another neighbor, and they had a small child.

Justin grabbed the shower curtain and wrapped it

around his body. "It's hailing pretty bad. I had to break down the shower door to help an elderly lady and her grandkids out of their house. The tornado hit over by my mom's house too," he continued. "I'm worried about my mom and grandma."

The sky was lightening, and Kayla could see more people out and about, helping others out of the debris. "Go check on them, Justin."

"I will. As soon as I'm done here." Holding the shower curtain around himself, he hurried off to help more people.

Cara Edens' Home

Most of the tenants in Cara's apartment building stood outside, surveying the clouds and sky as if hoping for answers. Golf ball-sized hail clanged against the wooden planks. The trees, still mostly bare with only small springtime leaves opening, did little to protect the apartments. Cara squinted through the branches. Big black clouds filled the sky to the east, looking like she imagined a hurricane would.

"Look." She nudged Stephen and pointed to the southwest. "See those big clouds?"

"Yeah." His eyes followed her finger. "Looks like a really bad thunderstorm. Like the worst ever."

"At least it's not over us." This storm made her nervous. "Come on, I'm going in."

Stephen followed her. Cara closed the patio door, popping her knuckles again. She sat back down on the couch, folding her knees up to her chest. If there was a tornado, it didn't have a set course and could change directions at any moment. There was nowhere for her to go and nothing to do but wait.

The Jason Residence

Penny grabbed at her hair as guilt riddled her. "We're

91

being punished. This is our fault for not going to church today!"

Pierre grunted as he slammed his whole body into the bathroom door.

"The couch," Penny whispered, her eyes riveted over his shoulder. She watched pieces of the front room swirl away. Walls, pictures, and insulation flew past. The wind howled around them, louder than a freight train roaring past.

The door shut with a click, and Pierre leaned against it, panting. Something splintered above them, and Penny covered her head with her arms, burying her face in Pierre's chest. The ceiling caved in, falling all around them. Penny screamed, but even she couldn't hear her own voice over the sound of the house splintering to pieces. *We're not making it through this.* This was it. They were going to die.

Where were her kids? Pierre's daughter? "I'm so sorry I didn't go to church today, Lord," Penny cried. Her whole body trembled, and she felt Pierre's arm around her, holding her close. Could his heart handle this? Was her son delivering pizzas right now, as he usually did on Sundays? She pictured the storm picking up his car and flying him through the air, pizzas and all. She sobbed, tears rolling down her cheeks one after the other.

And her mother at the senior building. She lived on the sixth of eight floors. Her main means of transportation was a wheelchair with an oxygen tank attached.

The door they leaned on collapsed, and both of them toppled to the ground. Penny felt the wind grab her legs and start to lift her, and then it dropped her on top of Pierre. "Oh, Lord, oh Lord!" Penny uttered the words in a panic and hoped the Lord would accept her heartfelt prayer. "I'm so sorry, I'm so sorry."

The Mitchells

"If you are missing family members or friends, you can call us," the radio announcer said. "Tell us what you see, what's happening now."

The newscaster was still speaking, so Joplin was still there. Why couldn't Nellie reach anyone?

Cade ran upstairs and came back down a moment later. "Nothing outside. It's not even raining. Looks like the storm passed us by."

Nellie sank into a chair, her fingers tingling. "What's going on out there? What's happening?"

The newscaster spoke again. "I'm going outside. I'm going to drive around town and report what I see."

Nellie shut her mouth and leaned forward, anxious to hear his report.

"I'm on Range Line. I'm driving down the street, and —" his voice choked up. "It's gone. It's all gone. IHOP is gone, the Goodwill's gone. Chick-fil-A's gone. Home Depot, Walmart…it's all gone. The devastation is incredible…. Range Line is barely recognizable."

Nellie looked at James. "What's he talking about? That can't be right." She couldn't even fathom one of the main streets in town without those businesses on it.

Nellie's phone dinged and she jumped. She'd almost given up expecting a response from anyone.

It was from Morgan. "My house hit."

Nellie swallowed past a sudden lump in her throat. She texted back, "Range Line is gone." Blinking, she met James's eyes. "Morgan's house was hit. This is bad, James."

He grabbed her hand, squeezed it. "I know. They're going to need me at work." James worked at Landmark, a hospital in Joplin for the chronically ill, those on ventilators, or people preparing to enter assisted living and permanent care.

James's phone rang. He pulled it out and answered it. "Dad. Are you okay?"

Nellie could hear her father-in-law's voice through the cell phone. "I'm fine, my house is fine. But the tornado must have hit a house near here. I was just standing in the dining room, watching out the window, and a piece of insulation hit the window."

Nellie stood up, thinking suddenly of her elderly mother who lived alone. She lived only two blocks south of Morgan. "We need to check on Mom. If Morgan's house was hit, hers could've been too."

"It can't be as bad as they all say."

Nellie tried calling her mother. After a moment, she shook her head and hung up. "Just getting a busy signal. She only has a landline. I bet the phone lines are down."

James clapped Cade on the shoulder. "We gotta go, man."

"Go, go," Cade said. "I'll take care of the film."

Nellie didn't wait for permission. She hurried out to the curb and started the car.

Melinda and Richard Borup

Melinda opened her eyes from their prayer and pressed a hand to her mouth, hardly able to believe what she saw.

Everything outside swirled around them. It wasn't just wind. A whirling vortex formed around the car, with leaves, debris, and other objects spinning past them. A large piece of sheet metal slammed into the concrete next to the car, and sparks flew. A tree fell in front of them, and the violence astonished Melinda. It didn't fall with a creak like in the movies. This fell like a giant had picked it up and slammed it to the ground. The car actually shook with the force of it.

Another tree slammed down behind them, then another, and another.

Melinda's hands shook and she pulled out her cell phone. They were going to die. She knew it. She started a text message to David, and words failed her. She'd always thought she'd know what to say in a moment like this. She typed out, "Oh, David, we're in a tornado," and hit send. Understatement of the year.

Screams filled the car, and Melinda wanted to cover her

ears with her hands, but she didn't seem to have control over her body. The wind and the swirling went on and on.

Then everything stopped. Melinda took several deep breaths, hot tears rolling down her cheeks. "What just happened?" she whispered.

"It's over," Richard said, unclenching the door handle.

Melinda turned to her son, taking in his pale face and sweaty brow. "You just screamed and screamed."

He shook his head. "No, Mom. That was you."

"That was me?" Melinda could hardly believe that horrible sound had come from her. She looked out the window next to her. Though the car had shaken through the entire storm, not once had it lifted off the ground. The top limb of the tree that had fallen next to her brushed the roof of the car, but none of the other trees had touched them. Neither had any of the debris.

The cars on the street around them had been tousled about like the many trees strewn so close to their vehicle. Many lay on their sides, and almost all had windows blown out. The houses around them had trees through them and roofs blown off. Somehow, they had come out unscathed. In front of them was a clear path just wide enough for a car to get through.

Melinda and Richard sat in stunned silence for several minutes.

"Well," Melinda said, turning the car back on, "I guess we should go home now."

Chapter Seven

Sunday, May 22, 2011
Approximately thirty minutes after tornado strike

"It took us over an hour to get to Joplin after we left I-44. The entire way was two-lane country roads. We were listening to the radio and there were storms all around us: a tornado in McDonald County, a tornado spotted in Newton County — right where we were. Right where we were going." — Tommie K. Ava

The Divine Household

Piper crossed back into Missouri around six p.m. Traffic worsened the closer they got to Joplin. An Oklahoma state trooper stayed in front of them, occasionally signaling all the cars behind him to pull over to the shoulder. He never got out of the car, and eventually he'd turn off his lights and Piper and the other cars would get back into the flow of traffic.

"What does he want?" Piper exclaimed after the fifth or sixth time.

Michael shrugged. "I don't know, Mom. But there's lots of cars out here."

By this time the cars trying to get into Joplin had formed a line. The vehicles inched forward, rain still pelting them.

"Ah," Piper whispered. "I bet the policeman is trying to keep us out of the storm. He's making us wait it out."

The McMinn Family

People began to stream by Kayla's demolished house.

96

"You need to come out of the bathtub," several said as they walked by. Kayla ignored them.

"Are you hurt?" someone else asked. Kayla shook her head but didn't budge.

Two teenage boys came over. They shoved the broken wall away from the tub. One knelt beside her. "You need to get your kids out of here. People who aren't injured are going to the park."

Kayla focused on him. "We're staying in the bathtub in case it comes back."

"If it comes back, you'll die. There's nothing left to shelter you."

Still Kayla didn't want to leave. "I'm waiting for my dad." He was coming, right? She'd called him and told him to come.

An older man came up beside the boys. "There's a gas leak, honey, right behind your house," the man said, his old eyes gentle. "The whole block could blow up."

Finally Kayla stirred. "Okay."

The man helped her lift Clark and Clayton out of the tub. Clayton shrieked and cried, reaching his hands toward the bathtub.

Clark began to cry also. "Where are you taking my brother? Don't take him!" He thrust one leg over the side of the bathtub and hurdled out.

"Clark, it's okay!" Kayla exclaimed. "We're not going anywhere! This nice old man's just helping us! Can you grab the baby's blanket?" She tried to calm her son by giving him an assignment.

Clark grabbed it and handed it to Clayton. The baby calmed down, resting his head on the soft fabric. Kayla handed Clark his Scooby Doo book, which he tucked under his arm. The man helped carry them past the debris of the demolished house, with Kayla trying not to look at the destruction.

"Thank you," she said. She looked across the street. Holding each boy tightly by the hand, they walked over to

97

the park. Kayla sat with them on a bench, just watching the flurry of activity around them.

"Excuse me."

Kayla looked at the woman who bent next to her. Two grungy men flanked her on either side. "Yes?"

"Do you know of any place where children might be trapped?"

The woman spoke softly, with caution in her voice.

"Yes," Kayla said, thinking of Stephanie. "I do. Our neighbors haven't been found. They have a little boy. They might be buried somewhere."

"I have some men who want to help." She gestured to the two men behind her. "Can you show them the house? It will only take a second. I'll stay with your children."

Kayla didn't want to leave her boys, but she could do this small thing to help. "Okay."

She led the men toward Stephanie's house. They were almost there when Kayla saw a flash of pink in the grass. She turned her head just a little and stifled a gasp. A little girl lay there. Kayla froze, taking in the twisted bodies lying in the ditch in front of her. She recognized both of them as belonging to another neighbor. Deep gashes and cuts packed with debris covered the little girl's body; blood pooled beneath her small, twisted frame. Her eyes were half-open, only showing the whites, and she didn't move at all. Dead. Kayla pressed a hand to her mouth, fighting nausea. She would've thought that the little boy was dead, too, from the way his body lay, but his chest rose and fell slightly.

Paramedics and other neighbors already scurried around the children. The men with Kayla left her side. At least Kayla didn't have to find help. One man tried to find a pulse on the little girl. Another lifted the boy gently even as his eyes slid closed.

"That boy's dead," a man said to the one holding the boy.

The other shook his head. "No, he's not. He's breathing.

We need a doctor."

"I'm a doctor." A tall man in jeans and a polo shirt stepped up. Kayla could tell he'd been in the middle of helping; blood and dirt stained his pants. "Someone said I should come over here."

They handed the little boy to the doctor. "He's alive," the doctor reported. "We need to get him to the emergency room."

"I'll take him." They transferred the boy carefully to another man's arms. "I just came from his house. I tried to notify his mom, but I couldn't find her."

"Just go." The doctor waved him off. "We'll find his parents later."

Kayla couldn't begin to process what she'd seen. "Justin!" she shouted. She scanned the wreckage around her, trying to find her fiancé. She couldn't even remember what he was wearing. Noticing she was shaking uncontrollably, she clenched her fists together.

"Kayla!" Justin appeared out of what was left of Stephanie's house, just in front of her. "Are you all right?"

She pointed. "The children." Kayla trembled from head to toe. "I'm going back to the park. I left our kids with a woman there. As soon as you're done, come and get me and we'll go to your mom's."

"Be careful," he said.

She nodded and headed back the way she'd come. She passed by another woman, obviously dead. The woman still sat on her toilet, the entire thing having blown from her house to the sidewalk. The toilet was smashed between two cars with the woman's head on the ground. There weren't any paramedics around her, but since it was obvious that she was dead, Kayla assumed they were more concerned with the living who needed help.

Kayla couldn't take it anymore. She focused straight ahead, not wanting to see anything else.

TORNADO WARNING
The Borup Family

The closer to home Melinda and Richard got, the sadder she felt. They drove through neighborhoods with people everywhere and mass destruction all around them. Melinda drove faster, anxious to get home before the roads became even more congested.

She turned down the street to their neighborhood and breathed a sigh of relief. Every house looked intact. The trees had a comical, cartoonish appearance: the leaves had all been blown off, leaving bare, stick figure branches to dance in the wind.

Melinda parked the car in the driveway, not even bothering with the garage. She bolted into the house through the porch door, entering via the kitchen. "David? David?"

David came into the kitchen, concern creasing his brow. "Mel? What's wrong?"

Melinda wrapped her arms around his waist and buried her face in his chest. "The tornado. We were in the tornado. Oh, David, it was awful!"

"What?" David pulled her head back and studied her. "What do you mean?"

Melinda used her hands to try to explain. "The wind. Lots of it, swirling around our car."

"It was probably just a straight line wind. Let's go look at your car."

"No, honey," Melinda said, beginning to feel exasperated. "It was a tornado. It was spinning in a circular motion."

She could tell David didn't believe her. "Show me the car. I want to see what happened."

She shrugged and led him out the door. "There's nothing to see. We didn't get hit by anything."

"I was there, Dad," Richard piped up, trailing them outside. "We were in the tornado."

David didn't reply. He let Melinda lead him to the car.

"There." Melinda pointed. "See? We were in it."

A single shingle stuck out of the car grill. David knelt to examine it. "Well, you're right. It had to be a strong wind to make that stick there."

"A tornado," Melinda supplied, folding her arms across her body.

"Maybe," David conceded.

Rain still fell, though not quite as torrential as before. "Let's get back in," Melinda said. She still felt too relieved to be alive to be annoyed with her husband.

They stepped into the house, and her teenage daughter Jessica came down the stairs, sobbing. "Mom!" she cried. "Hannah's house is gone."

Hannah was Jessica's best friend. Melinda could only stare at her. "What do you mean?"

"Exactly what I said!" Jessica cried. "We have to go get her. Her house is gone!"

Melinda had seen houses with damage, missing roofs, trees through the sides. She couldn't comprehend one that was *gone*. Still, she snapped into action. "Okay. Let's get in the car."

"I'm coming," Richard said, following close behind.

The Scaggs Household

"Meg. Meg."

Meg looked up to see Scott squatting in front of her, a screaming baby Harris in his arms.

"Meg, are you all right?"

Meg saw the concern in his eyes and shook her head to clear it. Her mind buzzed like a dozen bees had moved in. Only then did she realize her entire body was shaking, Lizzie and Nick still clutched tightly in her grasp. "What happened?" she gasped between chattering teeth. "Is it over?" She could hardly believe they were all still alive and sitting in the laundry room.

"It's over, Meg." Scott stood up, pulling Meg to her feet. "We're all here."

The emotional relief in Scott's voice echoed what Meg felt, and suddenly it overwhelmed her. She sobbed and hugged her family close to her.

"I'll be back," Scott said, and he left the room.

Meg pushed a hand through her hair and spotted the five loads she'd been working on that day. She sat down in the middle of the heap and began folding. It felt right to have a purpose, something to do. She let her mind go numb while her hands performed the familiar motions of smooth, fold, smooth again.

Scott came in and checked on her. "It's safer in here. Stay here with the kids."

The children fidgeted, whispering and crawling over each other and crying. Meg pulled out her cell phone and called her sister.

"Hello?" Eileen answered.

"The house," Meg said, doing her best to sound strong and in control, "the house is gone."

"What?"

Meg could tell from the confusion in Eileen's voice that she didn't understand.

"The tornado took out our house, Eileen."

Eileen gasped. "Meg, no! There was a tornado? What? All we got over here was a lot of rain and loud noise."

Meg nodded. "You're on the other side of town. It wiped us out over here."

"Oh, Meg! I'll be right there!"

Meg hung up the phone and started folding again.

The Mitchells

It seemed half of Missouri was driving to Joplin with Nellie and James. Traffic slowed as they neared the city. James took the Joplin exit and came to a stop as people walked in every direction. He inched the car forward.

Nellie hadn't paid any attention to the drive. She'd been busy texting people and trying to make phone calls. Only half of them seemed to be going through.

But as they drove through Joplin, Nellie couldn't resist looking around. The damage was every bit as bad as the radio announcer had made it sound. They reached 20th Street and James tried to go south, but every direction was completely blocked with debris, trees, or traffic.

"Nellie, I don't think I can get through to your mom's house," James said.

"Keep trying. We'll find a way through." Nellie squeezed James's hand as he drove. She knew they'd have a lot to do in the next few days, but she felt calm. They might not even have a house left. They had no choice but to tackle each obstacle head-on.

"Do you think the house is okay?" James asked, as if echoing her thoughts.

"I don't know," Nellie replied, fingering her phone. "I never heard back from Kevin."

"Hmm." James nodded. "I wonder what work will be like."

"Crazy," Nellie said. "You'll be needed a lot for a while. I hope my mom's okay."

"We'll get everything straightened out." James glanced at her before turning his attention back to the slowed traffic. "I'll go by the hospital after we get your mom."

"And we can check on our house, too."

"Yeah."

Almost every street they turned down was blocked. Cars idled and people stood everywhere, some helping, others gawking. It took about forty minutes, but they reached Nellie's mom's neighborhood.

Trees were down on the street. Nellie's mom lived on a dead end, and there was no way to get by. Cars turned around at the roadblock, seeking another way in.

"I can see her apartment complex," James said, exhaling. "It's still there. She must be okay."

Nellie searched the crowded street. "There's no place to park here. But we can park somewhere else and walk back."

"It will take hours," James said.

"We should try."

"We're both in flip-flops. We'll be trying to cross tree limbs and downed power lines."

Nellie knew he was right, but none of that mattered. "We have to try."

"Let's go to our house, Nellie. I saw an open road in that direction. Then we'll set out for your mom's house on foot." He turned the car around, following everyone else as they went back down the road.

Nellie's phone rang, and she answered it without checking the caller. "Hello?"

"Nellie?" Her cousin Debra burst into tears on the other end. "You're okay?"

Debra lived in Hawaii, and Nellie couldn't help feeling surprised that she already knew about this. "We're fine, Debra. How did you know?"

"I'm watching on The Weather Channel," Debra sobbed. "It's awful, Nellie. So awful. Are you sure you're okay?"

"I'm okay, I'm okay. What are they saying on the news, Debra?"

"All about the south side of Joplin being destroyed… people missing…dead."

"Calm down, Debra. We're fine. We weren't even in Joplin." The call waiting beeped, and Nellie checked it. Her aunt. "I've got to go, Debra. I'll call you soon." She clicked over. "Aunt Rebecca?"

"Nellie! Are you all right?"

"Yes. Hey, I'm so glad you called. I've been trying to reach my dad, but I can't. Can you call him for me?"

"Of course, Nellie. What do you want me to say? Is everything okay?"

Nellie wanted to scream, *No, of course it's not!* Instead, she said, "Tell him we're going to Mom's house. I'm okay."

She hung up the phone just as her brother in Arizona called. "Nellie, thank goodness. Why haven't you responded to my texts?"

"I didn't get them." Nellie checked her phone just to make sure. "It's sporadic right now."

"How's Mom?"

"Her house is still there. But we haven't been able to get to her."

"You've got to check on Mom. I can't reach her."

"Bryan, it's difficult here. I'm trying." Now everyone was calling. Nellie checked the call waiting; her brother-in-law this time. "We'll talk later. Hello?"

"Why isn't James answering his phone?" were the first words out of Dwain's mouth.

Nellie glanced at James, who pulled his phone out and examined it.

"It didn't ring," he said.

"He didn't know you called. Are you all right?" Nellie asked.

Dwain exhaled. "Yes. I just walked by your house. It's fine."

A tightness lifted from Nellie's chest. She'd been so intent on getting to her mother that she'd refused to think too much about her own house. "Thank you."

Cara Edens' Home

Cara went back and forth between staring out the patio door to pacing the apartment. She popped her knuckles profusely, wishing she could do something proactive.

As suddenly as the storm had descended, the sun reappeared. The air had a certain haze, as though the sunlight was streaming through droplets of rain. Cara relaxed her legs and went back outside. It must have been a quick spring shower—coming in, drenching everything, then leaving. She tried the landline phone. Still no dial tone. She couldn't get the cable for the Internet or TV to work either, but the electricity was back on.

"Glad that's over." Stephen got off the living room floor

and threw the pillows back on the couch. "I reek. I'm taking a shower."

He disappeared into the bathroom, and Cara retrieved her cell phone. She knew her dad would be calling soon to tell her it was over, so she figured she'd call first.

Mr. Edens' cell phone rang four times before going to voicemail. Cara tried again but got the same response. *Be calm,* she told herself, trying not to become unnerved. *The battery could be dead. Or…something.*

She tried the landline. This time not even the answering machine picked up; all she got was a busy signal. Cara's fingers trembled and she ran to the bathroom door. "Stephen!" she yelled, pounding on it, "you need to get out!"

Stephen stopped singing to himself. "What's wrong?"

"I can't reach my parents!" Cara's hands shook as she dialed her friend Emily, who lived close to the Edens. Again, only a busy signal. Emily and her husband had a small baby girl, and Cara felt a wave of nausea. What if something had happened to them?

Stephen came out, wearing a fresh pair of jeans and a T-shirt. "What's going on?"

"I can't reach anyone." Cara choked back tears.

Stephen took Cara's phone from her just as it rang. Cara snatched it back.

"Hello?"

"Cara, are you okay?" Cara's sister's voice carried through the phone line. "Did the tornado hit you?"

"Tornado?" Cara gasped. "It was just rain!" Out of her peripheral vision, she saw Stephen lean in closer, trying to catch Julie's words.

"It was a tornado," Julie confirmed. "And I can't reach Mom and Dad."

Or baby Caleb. The thought hit Cara like a ton of bricks, and she knew Julie had to be thinking about her son. Cara's heart sank. "We're leaving the house right now. Are you at work?" Today was Julie's first day at the restaurant.

"Yes," she said. "I'm looking for a ride. My car's wrecked. I'll be there soon."

Julie's voice caught, and Cara said, "We'll see you, then." She hung up before she cried on the phone. She was still wearing her tank top and sweatpants. Hurrying into the bedroom, Cara grabbed a jacket and threw on some yoga pants and a T-shirt. "Let's go, Stephen. We have to check on my parents."

"Change your flip-flops," he said, forcing his feet into tennis shoes. "You don't know what it'll be like out there."

The cell phones started ringing like crazy. First Stephen's mom called, and Stephen had to assure her he was okay. Cara's cousins called, but Cara was too distracted to talk. All she could think about were her parents.

The Jason Residence

The noise ended. The rattling halted, though debris continued to fall on them. Penny lifted her head and glanced around her. "Is it over?" she whispered. Why couldn't she see anything? Everything was dark. Somehow her glasses were still on; she reached a hand up and felt her face. No blood. Was she blind? She shivered, her wet clothes clinging to her frame. "Pierre?" Penny felt panic swelling again. "Pierre?" Why didn't he answer?

Pierre groaned and moved beneath her. His arm shifted, and Penny realized he still had it around her. "Penny. Are you all right?"

She burst into tears and leaned her head against him. "We're alive, Pierre." Gratitude welled up inside her and she sobbed, trying her best to get an arm under him and hug him.

He gave her a big one-armed squeeze and stroked her short hair. "It's going to be okay. I'm sure the kids are all okay." He sucked in a breath and groaned.

Penny jerked up. "Are you hurt?"

"I'm lying on something sharp. It's digging into my back

107

and thighs. Need to get up."

"I can't see anything." Even as she said it, Penny discerned shapes in the darkness she hadn't noticed before.

"I see a light," Pierre said. "We're buried. I need you to get off me so I can dig toward the light."

Penny reached out her hands and realized she still clutched her cell phone. Shoving it into her pajama pocket, she put her hands in front of her and pushed objects out of the way. More confident with every move, she lifted her head and spotted the sliver of light Pierre had seen. She balanced her foot on an uneven surface and reached up. "I can get there, Pierre." Her hands brushed at the opening and she shoved it wider.

"Good, because I can't."

Penny stopped and turned back to Pierre, frowning. "What do you mean?" She tried to push back the anxiety that was so near the surface of her emotions.

"Something's on my legs. I can't move them."

"I need to see." Penny climbed higher, finding the sink and lifting herself up. The ceiling was gone, and she moved enough debris to spill light down on them. Dropping down again, she saw clearly why Pierre was stuck. "You're under the washer and dryer." How the machines had traveled from the kitchen to the downstairs bathroom was beyond her, but there they were. "I'll try to get them off." She spotted the hot water heater a little behind Pierre's head and shuddered. Thank the Lord that hadn't landed on him.

Saying a quick prayer and summoning all her strength, Penny lifted the dryer enough to drag it off Pierre's legs. But all her grunting and sweating wasn't enough to lift the washer. She took a breather, gasping and wiping at the beads of sweat on her forehead.

"Pierre, I'm going to get help." She gripped his hands and squeezed, hating to leave him. "I can't get this off you by myself."

"Go on." He squeezed back. "I'm not going anywhere."

Her heart in her throat, Penny climbed back on the sink.

She got a good hold on something solid above the bathroom and shimmied herself through the opening. Sunlight, bright and inappropriate after such a storm, rained down on her. Penny blinked several times and pushed herself to her feet.

Her house was destroyed; all the walls were gone. The floor separating the basement and living room had blown away, and furniture from upstairs littered the basement haphazardly as if a giant had tossed them about in a tantrum. The four corners of the house were intact, but almost nothing remained between them.

For that matter, the entire street was leveled. "My Lord," Penny whispered, taking in the downed trees and devastation. It looked like a war zone.

"Penny!"

She blinked and turned in the direction of the shout. Her neighbor Tom and his daughter waved from across the street. Their own house lay in a heap of rubble, but the two of them hurried over to Penny.

"Are you all right?" he asked. "Do you need help?"

"I'm all right," she whispered, shaken again by the destruction around her. "But Pierre's stuck. I need help getting the washing machine off him."

Tom exchanged a look with his daughter. "We'll do what we can."

Chapter Eight

**Sunday evening, May 22, 2011
Approximately one hour after tornado strike**

"On the corner of 26th and Joplin, a car was twisted around the traffic light pole. It was HORRIBLE." — Tommie K. Ava

The Borup Family

Melinda had underestimated the amount of traffic there'd be. Hannah lived in the eastern area of Joplin, and the closer they got, the worse the devastation. Melinda drove down 32nd Street, aware of the gasps of shock coming from her children. She pulled out her camera and snapped a few photos of the destruction.

She turned down Range Line and almost stopped the car. It was like a bomb had exploded beneath the street, destroying everything aboveground. The sight stunned Melinda. There were people and cars everywhere. Home Depot, Target, Walmart... they were all gone. Pedestrians gawked or ran around aimlessly.

"I want a picture of the flag." The United States flag still hung from the flagpole. Richard took the camera from her and took a picture.

The car inched forward, but Melinda could tell they weren't going to get anywhere. Downed power lines lay across sidewalks, forcing people to walk in the street. Everyone seemed to be going somewhere.

"All right." Melinda turned into what used to be the Walmart parking lot and stopped the car. "We'll have to walk from here. We'll never get past this crowd."

The McMinn Family

"Kayla?"

A male voice aroused Kayla from her stupor. She looked up to see a friend of Justin's family standing in front of the park bench.

"Rob!" She stood up, holding her two boys by the hand. "Are you injured?"

He shook his head. "My house is fine. Why don't you and the kids wait with my girlfriend until Justin is done?"

"Yes," Kayla breathed, glad to get indoors. A steady drizzle had started after the tornado, and Kayla couldn't seem to get warm no matter how hard she tried.

"Are any of you hurt?" He looked over her and the boys.

"The baby." Kayla held up Clayton's leg. "He hurt it."

"I'll check it out. I'm an ex-cop and army vet."

A block from the park, the houses all looked perfectly intact. The tornado appeared to have passed them by. Rob ushered her and the children inside. "Debbie!" he called. "We've got company." Turning to Kayla, he said, "Stay with her. I'll find Justin."

Debbie came out of the bathroom, her eyes red. "Kayla, you're all right. What about your family?"

With the children quietly playing, Kayla felt like she could relax. She sank into the couch and stared at the wall. "We're fine, me and Justin. I don't know about my parents or his." Had anyone found Stephanie and her family?

And what about her own family? Kayla had no idea how they were.

Debbie sat next to her on the couch. "The tornado destroyed everything by Justin's mom's house," she whispered. "I hope his family is okay."

Kayla closed her eyes and shuddered. She hoped so, too.

She felt like she sat in that house for hours, but it was still light outside when Justin found her.

"Go back to the house and find some coats for us," Justin said. "It's still raining and it's getting cold. I've got to keep helping people. Your dad's here, too."

Kayla left the children with Debbie and headed back home. She stepped up to the remains and spotted her father standing in the driveway. With a sob, Kayla ran to him. Never in her life had she felt so happy to see him as in that moment. No matter what had happened, everything would be fine now that he was here.

He wrapped her up in a hug. "Are you okay? Are the kids okay?"

"Yes," Kayla cried. "Where were you? I was so scared! Why weren't you here?"

He smoothed her hair. "Honey, I had no idea. I was still sleeping off the night shift. I didn't even hear about it until after five. Your sister called me and told me a tornado hit Joplin. I came as quickly as I could. I took the back way to Seventh Street, but I stopped at Walmart for a few things and from there everything looked fine. I called your mom, and she said it didn't look like the tornado had touched down. I thought maybe it had just hit outside of town. It wasn't until I got closer that I realized it had hit the town. And then I saw your house." He took a deep breath. "I called the police commissioner to see if he'd heard from you. I feared the worst, Kayla, especially when none of you were here." He clenched his jaw. "I didn't think anyone could've survived that. That's when Justin came running up."

Justin joined them. "I found your dad standing over the bathtub, crying into the phone that we were all dead." He shook his head. "We're alive. But we lost our car. I really want to check on my mom. Can you take us?"

Kayla's father nodded. "Of course."

"Let me just get a few things first," Kayla said. She grabbed another pair of shoes that didn't appear too damaged. She found a pair of Clark's also, but not Justin's.

The PlayStation lay on its side on the sidewalk. Kayla picked it up and poked at the buttons. It looked like it might still work. She tossed it into the car, then thought of the memory box she had for their stillborn son, Brad. She couldn't leave that behind. "Justin, keep an eye out for Brad's box, okay?"

He gave the rubbish a quick once-over. "I'll look later, Kayla. Let's go."

They piled into her dad's car. Kayla hadn't realized her stepmom was there too, but the woman quickly embraced her. Justin said, "We forgot jackets."

"Let me grab the kids," Kayla started to open the door.

"I'll pick them up," her dad said. "Where are they?"

"At Rob's house."

"Stay put. We'll get them as soon as Justin gets in the car."

Kayla settled back and waited with her dad, enjoying the warmth of the heater, while Justin searched the debris for dry clothes and jackets.

The Scaggs Household

It seemed only a second had passed when Scott came back, her father in tow.

"You're dad's here," he said. "There's a way out through the garage." Scott grabbed Meg's hand and squeezed hard. "Meg, you get out of here with the kids, but I need to stay. This is bad. This is really, really bad."

"Okay," Meg whispered, meeting his eyes. She didn't want to be away from him right now, but she knew she couldn't convince him otherwise.

"Come on, honey." Meg's father put her on her feet.

The top of the house was gone, but the stairs leading up to the garage were intact. Meg instructed the kids to hold each other's hands and they stepped outside.

She stopped where her porch had been and stared. The entire block was leveled. A few walls stood haphazardly with no rhyme or reason, but mostly she could see straight through to the streets several blocks away.

Besides the stairs to the basement, all that was left of

their house was the master bedroom. The living, dining, and other rooms had been completely taken out. Blobs of insulation, chunks of dirt, and broken glass and drywall littered what remained.

Meg straightened her shoulders. She could see pieces of furniture, books, pictures, and cookware buried in the ruble. As much as she felt like curling up and crying, she knew they needed to save as much as they could, and quickly. Rain still poured steadily from the sky, drenching everything exposed.

"What happened, Mom?" Lizzie asked, her eyes wide as she turned in a circle, examining their house.

"A tornado, honey," Meg said, wondering how on earth she would explain this to a child. "Lots of wind. It picked up our stuff and threw it around."

"Tornado?" Lizzie echoed. "It looks like it pooped everywhere."

"Pooped," Nick said, giggling.

"Tornado poop," Lizzie repeated, and the children laughed. Even Meg smiled. The nickname stuck, and it helped lighten the tension.

Meg found an old box that had survived the tornado, and she began piling picture frames and kitchen objects into it.

The Divine Household

It took an hour and fifteen minutes to get to the Schifferdecker exit.

"Finally," Piper said, taking it.

She knew Range Line had suffered damage. She didn't expect the damage to extend this far west. Piper got as far as 32nd Street before the military police stopped her.

"You can't come this way," the officer said.

"But this is how I get home," Piper protested.

"You'll have to get back on the interstate and take the next exit."

More alarmed than frustrated, Piper pulled back onto the interstate. She took the Main Street exit, again heading down 32nd to get to Maiden Lane. Traffic forced her to stop at 32nd and Wall Street. The truck in front of her had a young kid driving, maybe twenty-five or twenty-six years old. He was trying to turn north, but a downed tree blocked him. Everyone behind him sat and waited while he pulled out a chainsaw and hacked up the tree.

Piper didn't really mind. She could take that street, and maybe get out of this traffic jam. Once he cleared the tree, she followed him, continuing north.

When she got to 26th Street, though, things started backing up again. Piper tapped her fingers on the steering wheel, trying not to be impatient. It wasn't easy after being in the car for hours. She checked on her son in the rear view mirror. "You doing okay back there, Michael?"

"Uh-huh," he said, not even looking up from his book.

Well, at least she didn't have to worry about him.

Piper had a sudden thought. *Ashley. Ashley's husband is a firefighter.* She racked her brain, trying to remember if Ashley had mentioned him being on duty that day. She pulled out her phone and tried to call her, but there was no answer.

Ashley had been out shopping earlier. Had she been in this?

She suddenly had the unnerving feeling of being lost. "Where am I?" she murmured. She saw a church and a parking lot across the street and thought she must be on 20th Street. "How odd," she said aloud. "I thought I was still on 26th."

"What, Mom?"

"Nothing. Just talking to myself." Piper flipped her blinker on and managed to turn around. Taco Bell rose up in front of her.

"What?" Piper exclaimed. Then this *was* 26th Street. But she didn't recognize it.

They drove past the body of a woman in the street. The

115

way she lay, haphazard and twisted, made Piper think she'd been thrown from a house. Police worked to remove the body of another woman dangling from a street sign, impaled by the metal rod. Piper gagged and pressed a hand to her mouth. The sight traumatized her. Seeing dead people in real life was totally different than seeing them on TV. Having her son so absorbed in a book was a blessing because he didn't see it. But it also meant she couldn't help anyone. She couldn't leave him alone. All Piper could do was stare ahead and pretend she hadn't seen anything.

Cara Edens' Home

The whole way to her parents' house, Cara tried her dad's cell phone over and over again. Every time the voicemail picked up, she felt her heart rate increase. She took a deep breath and dialed again.

"Hello?" Mrs. Edens' voice answered. She sounded far away and vacant, but at least she answered.

"Mom!" Cara blurted. "What's going on?"

"Cara," she said. "The house was destroyed."

The words didn't register with Cara. They just didn't make sense. "What?"

"It's completely gone. There's no more house."

For a moment Cara's mouth gaped open. Then she sputtered, "Are you guys okay?"

"We're okay," her mom said. "Me and your dad and Caleb are okay. Uncle Todd's here. He just showed up. He's helping us." Her mom's voice strengthened. "Don't come over here, Cara. There's too much going on. It's a wreck."

The tears that Cara had held back for the past half hour burst out of her. Cara had grown up in that house; they'd moved there when she was two years old. The thought that it was gone was devastating. She'd moved out not even a year ago, at the age of twenty-two. It didn't seem real.

"We'll be there soon, Mom," Cara sobbed, ignoring her mom's orders to stay put.

"Which way are we going?" Stephen asked as soon as Cara was off the phone.

Cara always knew the shortcut or backroad to get somewhere. She learned it from her dad, who believed he could get somewhere faster if he avoided main roads.

"Take Florida to 15th Street," she directed.

She could hardly believe what she saw as they drove. Downed tree limbs littered the street. Looking west, Cara saw what used to be a big church on 15th. They continued driving, and Cara saw that everything on Connecticut Street had been destroyed. The whole east side was gone. People were outside, looking around, dazed expressions on their faces. Nobody seemed to fully comprehend what had happened.

Her parents lived by St. John's Hospital. Cara closed her eyes. How had it gotten this far?

"Cara," Stephen said, drawing her out of her reverie, "the road's blocked by trees. We need a different way."

"Okay." Cara took a deep breath and mentally planned a different route. Several more times they had to change course as they were met by downed power lines, trees, and lots of other people trying to get to their families.

The Jason Residence

Penny and her neighbor, Tom, widened the hole leading to the bathroom and dropped back in to Pierre.

"Glad to see you didn't forget me," Pierre said.

Penny gave him a smile. She helped her neighbor grip the heavy washer and heave it off his legs.

"Ahh," Pierre groaned. He lifted his pajama pant leg to reveal a deep cut.

"Oh, Pierre," Penny said. "We need to get that looked at."

"I'm okay." He extended a hand, and Penny and Tom helped him to his feet. Pierre glanced behind him. "Oh. The toilet. I wondered what was poking me."

Sure enough, the white porcelain toilet had broken into half a dozen pieces.

"The real question is, how did it get under you?" Penny tried to smile, though it wobbled frailly. She checked Pierre over for more cuts, but he brushed her off.

"I'm a bit bruised, but fine. Let's get out of here."

She studied his face and nodded, certain he wasn't lying. And somehow he still had his glasses, too.

Between Penny, Tom, and his daughter, they managed to get Pierre out of the rubble. Again Penny took in the sight of the flattened houses on their street, the stripped trees. People milled about in the road, confusion on their faces.

"There we are." Pierre settled himself on his feet and Penny watched him realize the extent of the devastation. "Wow," he whispered.

"Olivia, stay with Penny and Pierre," Tom said to his daughter. "I'm going to try and help."

Penny took the girl's hand, patted it. "You'll be fine with us."

Olivia nodded and gave a weak smile.

Penny's eyes widened, and her fingers flew to her left hand. "My wedding ring!" Her head turned to the master bedroom automatically, except, of course, it wasn't there.

Pierre's arm went around her shoulder. "It's all right. We're still here. But we need shoes."

Tears stung Penny's eyes, and she nodded. He was right. They couldn't traipse around this destruction barefoot. She cursed herself again for putting pajamas back on and skipping church.

"Look." Pierre pointed to the right. "The carport is still there."

Penny followed his gaze. Sure enough, the white Hyundai and Nissan were in the carport. But Penny knew they hadn't parked the cars facing each other, bumpers touching as if they were kissing. The hoods were gone, exposing the inner workings like a gutted beast. A tree lay on top of Pierre's Nissan and a big 2x4 stood straight out of the Hyundai's motor.

"Well." Pierre scratched his bald head. "Doesn't look like the cars are going anywhere."

Penny looked at him and burst out laughing. "No," she agreed, "I suppose not."

A light drizzle fell on them, and Pierre started limping toward the cars. "Watch your step, Penny."

Penny tiptoed behind him, clutching her cell phone like a life support. Olivia followed close behind. Pierre opened the car doors and began shifting through the clutter.

"I can't get a signal," Penny murmured, trying again to call her stepdaughter.

"I found shoes." Pierre dropped out four shoes, all different sizes and colors.

Penny's brow furrowed together. "You couldn't find a matching pair?"

"It's not important now, is it?" Pierre jammed his feet into the largest ones.

Penny wanted to laugh again. Her husband, the smart dresser, now wearing mismatched shoes.

"I'm going to help Tom," he said.

"You can't," Penny objected, fear lurching in her chest. "You're injured. What if the storm comes back?" As if to prove her words, lightning flashed nearby.

Pierre opened the back door of the Hyundai. "It's over, Penny. But there are people worse off than us. You and Livvy stay here in the car."

Penny wrapped an arm around Olivia, who had begun to shiver. "Okay. Please be careful, Pierre." Images of exposed utility cords and gas leaks filled her mind. "Come on, Livvy. Let's get inside."

"Do you need a blanket?"

Penny spun around as a lady her age approached them, lips pressed together with tension. She extended a thick comforter toward Penny.

"Don't you need it?" Penny asked, reluctant to take it

119

even as her hands reached for it, itching to wrap the warmth around her and Olivia.

The lady shook her head. "I'm looking for my husband. He was out by the Elk Lodge." She pointed behind the ruins of Penny's house. "Did you see him?"

Penny swallowed past a lump in her throat and shook her head. At least she had her husband with her. "No, ma'am, I didn't," she whispered. "I'll keep an eye out."

"Thank you. Take this blanket. Stay warm."

"Thank you." Penny ushered Olivia into the backseat and praised the Lord that she and Pierre were okay. Tears stung her eyes, and she brushed them away.

"I'll help look for him. Penny, I'll be back," Pierre said.

Penny nodded, not trying to dissuade him. He was right. They were better off than others.

The Mitchells

The direct route to Nellie and James's house was blocked. Power lines lay across the road, over sidewalks. Nellie saw people braving the debris, walking anyway. She still wore her flip-flops, though, and wasn't about to try it.

They drove around the long way, grateful to find a road that was open.

"There's our house." Nellie was never so happy to see the little spinner in the garden. The rainbow-colored petals spun in the wind, but it was intact. Several trees were down, but none of them had damaged the small, two-story stone house. The remaining trees were bare of leaves, empty limbs fluttering.

Nellie instantly felt calmer. She ran out of the car and through the screen door, letting it slam behind her. Darkness greeted her; she could barely make out the big screen TV in the living room next to the stone fireplace.

James came up behind her. Nellie tried the hall light—nothing. "I don't think we have electricity."

James opened the hall closet and pulled out a Maglite.

"Not a problem."

"I want to check on my mom." Nellie fumbled into the master bedroom and threw together a bag of clothing. She kicked off her flip-flops and put on tennis shoes.

"Here's the first-aid kit." James put it in a satchel and tossed it over a shoulder. "Ready when you are."

Nellie checked his shoes. He'd also put on tennis shoes. "Let's go, then."

Nellie and James jogged the two miles from their house to Nellie's mom's house. Nellie didn't consider herself or James athletic, but they had been committed to their gym membership this year. She'd dedicated herself to spin classes, Zumba, and running several times a week. Six months ago, she wouldn't have been able to run a block. But thanks to the gym membership, she was in better shape than she had been since high school.

As if to cement the notion, she spotted her junior high gym teacher running with his wife. "Hey, Coach!" she shouted.

"Nellie!" he called back.

Nellie knew he remembered her little brother more than he remembered her, since her brother went to his school, but they'd seen each other on occasion since she graduated.

He jogged next to them. "Where are you going?"

"We're trying to get to Moffet Street," Nellie said. "You?"

"We're just helping people. Take 26th over to Moffet. You won't be able to cut through the St. Mary's parking lot."

The fallen trees and debris made it more hazardous than normal, but James kept his flashlight on the trail in front of them, helping them see the way.

"I bet you wish you would've run more in junior high!" Coach joked.

"Well, I've been working out," Nellie said. "But...not so much into running!" Nor did she plan to be after this, either. Running was not her thing.

Coach and his wife pulled back. "Just keep going south.

121

We're going to head back north."

"Thanks," James said, waving the flashlight.

Nellie gasped at the damage some of the houses had sustained. She could hardly recognize the street, even though she drove through this neighborhood every single day, only a few blocks from her house. She thought of her students, scattered throughout the city, and hoped they were all okay.

Nellie reached 20th Street and stopped. She stood on the corner of the intersection and looked both ways.

"What's wrong?" James paused beside her.

"I can't even tell where I am," Nellie breathed. She couldn't believe her eyes. She knew where she should be. But she stared at the empty lot in front of her, not accepting that the elementary school was gone. "I can't be on the right street." She looked west, searching for a familiar landmark, but saw none. Turning to the east, she saw Taco Bell. "Taco Bell is still standing."

But nothing else was. The buildings around Taco Bell had been demolished, and the fast-food joint itself was trashed. She looked a little farther and saw St. John's Hospital.

At least she had a direction. She and James took off again. Their jog brought them closer to the hospital, and Nellie saw then that walls were missing from the multi-story building. All that was left was a shell. Fires flashed inside, and smoke rose from several different places.

Nellie forced herself to keep going. They ran past the nursing home behind her mom's complex. The tornado had leveled it. Nurses scurried about, trying to extricate patients.

Chapter Nine

"I watched bleeding people huddled together by the side of the road, wrapped in wet towels, crying." — *Michelle Short*

"Homes, the grocery store, the church just down the block — all gone or in such ruin [as] to be unrecognizable!" — *Diane Humphrey*

The Divine Household

It took forty minutes to go six blocks. Although both Piper and her mom lived on the north side of town, the route to their houses was right in the middle of everything that had happened. The tornado had destroyed the area, taking out familiar buildings and landmarks. Piper's hands shook. She just wanted to check on her mom and make sure the house was still there.

She tried her phone again, but her mom still didn't answer. This freaked her out. She didn't know if it meant her mom was injured, or if the phone lines were down. Text messaging was spotty; half of her texts weren't going through.

Piper's phone rang, startling her. She checked the number to see her brother calling. "Hello?" Piper said.

"Hey," he said. "You good?"

"Yeah, yeah," Piper said. "We're here in Joplin. Trying to get to Mom. Have you heard from her?"

"Yeah, actually," he said. "Just talked to her. She wanted me to call you and make sure you're okay. Said she can't get through to you."

Piper closed her eyes briefly in relief, then opened them and focused on traffic. "Same here. Tell her I'm on my way."

"Will do."

Piper battled the traffic a few more minutes when she saw the interstate on-ramp. She gave up on her mom's house and decided to go home. It might be faster to take the backroads route to her mom's from her house, anyway. Piper got off the city roads and back on the interstate. She took the 249 exit. Overturned semis littered the sides of the road. One truck hung over the bypass. A tow crew worked to remove the semi dangling over the road. Cars were thrown about. Tow trucks moved the vehicles to the median, or off to the side of the road. But even that wreckage didn't compare to the devastation she'd seen on Main and 26th.

The Borup Family

Melinda and the two teenagers had only walked a few hundred yards when Richard halted.

"Mom."

"What?" Melinda turned to him, concerned. She realized he hadn't bothered changing either, and still wore his concert clothes from graduation. "What's wrong?"

His brow wrinkled. "I was just thinking about the Bartows and the Wrights."

Melinda nodded. He referred to the two families from church he helped look after. She understood in an instant where he was going with this.

"I should check on them."

Melinda hesitated. She was reluctant to let her fifteen-year-old boy go off by himself in this wreckage. "Try calling them."

"Good idea."

They continued toward Hannah's house while Richard

dialed their numbers. "No answer. I'll try texting."

A moment later Richard stopped again. "I just heard from the Wrights. Both families' houses have been destroyed." Emotion twisted his boyish features. "They need me, Mom."

Melinda's heart sank and she took a deep breath. It was at least three miles from Range Line to their houses, and probably just as dangerous as it was here. But she knew the Wrights had a one-month-old baby and a small daughter. "All right. Go. But be careful. Wait there for me. I'll come get you guys."

"Thanks, Mom." Richard loosened the top button on his shirt and took off running.

The McMinn Family

Before they left the house, Kayla and Justin tried one last time to start their car. Though the roof was dented and the hood caved in, they hoped they could get it started.

"Nothing," Justin said, giving up.

They got back in Kayla's father's car. They had to park six blocks away from Justin's mom's house. The duplexes and apartments around them had been leveled, and Kayla couldn't imagine the two older women seeking cover. Kayla stayed in the car with the children while Justin jogged over to check on them. Half an hour later he was back, sliding into the backseat next to Kayla.

"How are they?" Kayla asked breathlessly, her heart pounding in anticipation.

"They're okay," Justin said. "The garage is destroyed and there are some broken windows, but they're fine. My sister, too."

Kayla exhaled. "That's a miracle."

"Do you have your phone?" her father asked, turning the car around.

Kayla automatically reached for her purse before realizing she didn't have it. "It's out of minutes. We'll have to go back to the house and get my purse." If she could even find it in the destruction.

It was dark by the time they returned to the house, and rummaging in the darkness made it even harder. But somehow Kayla found her purse, complete with the cell phone.

"Great," her dad said as she climbed back into the car. "I'm taking you guys to Walmart on 7th. It wasn't destroyed and you're gonna need some things."

"Yes," Kayla agreed, resting her head wearily against the window.

But when they pulled into the Walmart parking lot, they found it completely packed. Her father drove around several times looking for a parking spot before changing his mind. "Let's just go back to Miami. We'll go to the Walmart there."

The whole forty minute drive, her dad's phone rang nonstop with people wanting to know if he'd found Kayla; if everything was okay. He briefed everyone that called, then contacted his sergeant to say he would be late to work that night.

People stared at them in the Miami Walmart as they walked by. Kayla pushed a hand through her hair self-consciously. Did they look that bad? Some people shot her dirty looks and whispered loudly to their companions.

The behavior stung, especially since Kayla had just lost her house and everything in it. She tried to ignore them and went about her business. She needed stuff for the baby. She grabbed handfuls of bottles and clothing from the clearance rack, tossing it into the cart.

"Excuse me," a frail male voice said by Kayla's elbow, and she turned to see an older gentleman standing there.

"Yes?" Kayla asked cautiously, trying not to sound suspicious.

He gestured to her and the cart. "Were you in that tornado?"

Some of Kayla's guard dropped. "Yes."

"My daughter was in that storm too." He held out his hand and put twenty dollars into hers. "Take this, then. It's not much but I hope it helps. Good luck to you."

Kayla's fingers closed around the paper bill in her hand, and she stared at this stranger. "Thank you. Thank you for your generosity."

She watched him even after he walked away. That small gesture lifted her spirits and made her feel good inside.

Kayla's dad paid for her things. "I got you a phone card too," he said, handing her the small plastic card. "You need to activate your phone. It's no good in an emergency otherwise."

She couldn't agree more. "Thanks, Dad," Kayla said, taking the card.

The Scaggs Household

Meg's father piled the family into his car and drove them closer to the heart of Joplin.

"I just need to see how bad it is," he said.

Meg watched his hands clench and unclench the steering wheel. Her father was on the Joplin City Council, and she knew this must be horrible for him, to imagine the damage done to the city he loved so much.

Updates came across the radio, and the newscaster detailed the most damaged areas, what to do about missing people, and what roads were closed.

Meg's father didn't get very far. The streets were congested with cars going everywhere. He shook his head. "I'm just going to make it worse. These people have places they need to be. Let's go home."

Several ambulances zoomed by, sirens blaring. They fought the other cars for road space.

"I don't need the radio to tell me how bad it is," he said. "See those ambulances? They're from Kansas City and Springfield. They wouldn't be here if it wasn't really bad."

As they drove toward his house, the radio confirmed

127

what he'd said. Reports came in about St. John's Hospital being hit and destroyed, with the sick and injured being transferred to other hospitals.

The Mitchells

It had started raining again by the time they reached Nellie's mom's apartment complex. Several of the brick, single-story duplexes had been flattened. There was no clear path to her mom's apartment, not on the road or the walkway. Nellie fought back panic as she and James climbed over the debris of nearby houses.

Her mom's apartment was part of a quadplex. It was brick and on ground level, but built into a small hill. Two other apartments were directly below hers. Because of the hill, Nellie and James had to work their way upward. Getting past the debris, Nellie increased her speed and jogged around to the front, which faced away from the road, looking out over the nursing home behind the apartments.

Her mother sat on the curb in her pink pajamas with no shoes on, but had her purse on her shoulder, a dazed expression on her face. Her lapdog shivered in her arms. "Mom!" Nellie burst out, ecstatic with relief. Her eyes moved to the building behind her, and her stomach clenched. The entire apartment complex had collapsed. Somehow, her mother's building was still standing.

James reached her mother first. She gave him a huge hug, rocking him back and forth. Nellie put a hand on her mother's shoulder, her knees nearly giving way beneath her.

"Oh, Nellie." Her mom pulled back from James. Rainwater matted her gray hair, and she shook her head.

Joe, a friend of the family, stood with her. "Nellie, James, I'm so glad you're here," he said. "We need to move Elizabeth, but I need help."

Her mother and the dog were soaked, and rain still fell around them. "Why are you still here, Mom? Are you hurt?" Nellie crouched beside her. She knew her mom had a heart problem, but she would just have to walk through the debris. Already darkness descended upon them.

"No, no, I'm fine," her mom said, shying away from Nellie.

But Nellie caught sight of the bloody gash creeping up her mother's foot and calf. Though it had been wrapped in paper towels, she could see pieces of raw flesh hanging out. Nellie gasped. "What happened?"

"She was behind the apartment door when the tornado hit," Joe answered for her. "It blew open, and she tried to close it against the rain and hail. The tornado threw her across the room and she cut her foot."

"I can see that!" Nellie pulled at her hair, frantic. "She's going to bleed to death! It's getting dark. We can't just sit here!"

"We need to dry them off," James said, wiping his brow with his arm.

Joe shook his head. "I've already gone through the apartment. Northing's dry. The roof's blown off."

Unable to believe it, Nellie ran up the walk and threw open the door. Furniture lay on its side, broken ceiling and drywall littered the floor. The apartment was trashed.

Nellie pressed her hands to her mouth, trembling. She resisted the urge to go inside. "My paintings," she murmured. So many of her things were still at her mother's house. Things from school; some of her first artworks.

Now was not the time to worry about it. Nellie shoved it from her mind and hurried back to her mom. "Mom, we're going to find a way to get you out of here."

"What do you have in mind?" Joe crouched next to her mom, putting an arm around her shoulder.

Nellie blinked against the rain and scanned the lawn, hoping for inspiration. The nursing home caught her eye. Even from here she could see the nurses wheeling patients from the wrecked building. "I'll be right back."

Without waiting for a response, she took off for the

nursing home. When she reached it, she saw a woman pushing an empty wheelchair.

"Excuse me," Nellie said, stopping next to her. "Can I have this? My mom is hurt. I can't get her away from her apartment, she can't walk."

The woman squinted her eyes at Nellie. "That woman by the apartment buildings? I saw her just a few minutes ago. Yes, go ahead, you can use this."

"Thank you!" Nellie grasped the wheelchair handles and hurried back to the building.

"Here, Mom." She stepped back and let James and Joe put her mom in the chair. James had used the first-aid kit to redo her mother's bandage, this time with gauze and tape. Nellie pulled out her camera and snapped a few pictures of the wreckage around them. Her mother still clutched the little dog, her eyes glazed. Nellie feared she was in shock.

"I found a leash for the dog," Joe said. "Where am I going with her?"

"Back to the nursing home," Nellie said. "They had nurses and ambulances. They can help."

They started making their way to the parking lot of the nursing home. Several men ran out to meet them and helped lift the wheelchair over telephone poles, tree limbs, and wood strewn about the road. As soon as they wheeled her mother onto the nursing home property, paramedics descended upon them. Nellie stepped back while they moved her mom to an ambulance.

"She's losing too much blood," one paramedic said. "We need blood."

"Take her to the triage outside St. John's," another said. "They already have people donating."

Nellie turned in a circle, taking in the chaos around her. Smoke drifted from the building, nurses scurried about, and men shouted back and forth to one another. Fire burned near the back, and bloody people loped toward the ambulance. Volunteers and nurses helped as many as they could. More ambulance sirens blared in the distance,

130

though Nellie couldn't tell if they were en route to the nursing home or not.

"Nellie, come on!" James shouted.

She shook her head and hurried into the back of the ambulance. Nurses piled more injured people in and closed the doors. The sirens came on and the driver sped to the nearest hospital.

Cara Edens' Home

After forty-five minutes of driving, Stephen parked the car. "We're close enough," he said. "We'll walk from here."

Cara joined him, clutching his hand as they walked over and around debris. Her parents lived six blocks away. Pedestrians and cars covered the roads, the sidewalks, the grass. People searched for their families, or simply stood gawking. A few had cameras, recording the destruction.

"They're in the way," Cara said, pointing out the cars going only a few miles per hour, impeding those who were searching for family or trying to help. "They should take pictures later."

Stephen squeezed her hand but said nothing.

They avoided power lines, but easily jumped over insulation, broken glass, bricks, and trees. Dozens of obstacles marked the path to Cara's family's house.

Finally, Cara saw her dad. She kept her eyes glued to his face, not wanting to see what was left of the house. Her parents stood at the curb with baby Caleb next to Uncle Todd's pickup. Her nephew was wrapped in a hoodie, but Cara could tell from the way he leaned into her mom that he was cold.

Cara broke into a jog. She threw her arms around her dad, then hugged her mom and cried. She grabbed her nephew next, holding Caleb to her and rocking him.

"It's all right, Cara," her mom said, her voice hushed. "We're all okay."

Cara wiped her eyes and took a step back. She finally

lifted her eyes to the house, or rather, what remained. The shock of seeing the empty lot, covered with broken windows, pieces of roof, and chunks of cement, nearly knocked her over. It didn't seem real. It didn't seem like she was really looking at the house she'd grown up in. She saw her Uncle Todd in the wreckage. "What's he doing?"

Her mom turned around. "Searching for your dad's wallet. He lost it somewhere in there."

"How did Uncle Todd get here so fast?"

"He was one of the first people to get on the road after the tornado hit. He managed to find a route where there weren't downed power lines or backed-up traffic."

Cara stared at the house. She couldn't believe the destruction. Only two walls remained standing. "Nothing's left. Where were you guys?"

"In the hall closet." Cara's mom pointed to the small closet snuggled next to the remaining walls.

"All three of you?"

"Yes. Though your father almost didn't make it."

"Why?" Cara gasped, squeezing her fists together. "What happened?"

"Right after you called, he got out of the shower. He started hauling his hunting gear out of that closet and laying it out on the ground. I went and grabbed Caleb. Then your dad, just like always, went to the front door to watch the storm."

Cara groaned. She could imagine what was coming.

"Then we heard it. The roar. He told us to get into the closet, but he didn't budge. But this was bad." The skin around Cara's mom's eyes tightened. "I knew it. I begged him to come in with us, so he did. Just barely in time." She shook her head. "We still can't find the dog."

"Indie?" Cara glanced toward Stephen. He'd be sad to hear it. He and the little dog had a special connection. She turned in the direction of her friend Emily's house. Like most of the buildings on the block, it had been eradicated. Her heart lurched at the thought of them trying to save

132

TAMARA HART HEINER

themselves and their tiny baby girl. "Mom, did you see Emily?"

Her mother's brow crinkled. "No, honey, I didn't."

"Mom! Cara!"

Both women turned as Cara's sister Julie barreled down the sidewalk toward them. Two other women trailed her, moving at a slower pace. Julie's eyes swept past her mother and landed on Caleb. She gave a throaty cry and swept him into her arms.

"You're okay." She wrapped an arm around her mother. "You're all okay."

Her mom gave her a squeeze. "How was the first day on the job?"

Julie laughed and sobbed. She looked a lot like Cara, with pale skin and brown hair. But where Cara had green eyes, Julie's were brown. She took a step back and brushed at tears. "It was so slow. We only had one couple in the restaurant, and that was before the power went out." She gestured to the girls behind her. "They gave me a ride. We had no idea what we'd find. I think they came for moral support. I called Sam," she said, referring to her fiancé. "He should be here soon."

"Good." Their mother started back up the littered driveway. "We've got work to do."

The Jason Residence

After what seemed like hours, Pierre opened the back door to the car and stuck his head in. "You okay, Pen?"

Penny nodded, her arm still looped around Olivia. "What's going on out there?"

Pierre glanced at Tom, who hovered over his shoulder. "We did what we could. All our neighbors are okay. We found that lady's husband, the one who gave you the blanket." Pierre pointed at the comforter covering Penny.

"Oh, good." Penny let out a breath. "I was worried."

Pierre's brow furrowed. "He's dead, Pen. We found

him, that's all."

The breath rushed out of Penny. "Dear Lord," she whispered.

"But everyone else is okay," Tom said hurriedly. "Just a bit bruised and shook up real bad. All of us are."

Olivia leaned forward. "What about Mommy? Have you talked to her yet?"

Tom extended a hand to her and helped her from the car. "Phone's aren't working, baby. But it's light enough out still. Let's go find her."

Penny climbed out too, dropping the blanket on the seat. Her children's faces popped through her mind. She checked her cell phone again. Still no signal. She'd tried several times in the past hour. "Pierre, we need to find your daughter."

"I know," he said, his lips tight in a grim expression. "Ready to walk down Roosevelt?"

Penny glanced down at the two right shoes on her feet and grimaced. "Yes." At least she wasn't barefoot.

"Here." Pierre took off one of his giant shoes. "I happen to be wearing two left feet. Why don't we switch?"

"Great idea," she agreed. She stared down at the mismatched, ill-fitting shoes. "Thank you."

Pierre extended his hand. Penny slipped hers into his and they started down the street. The closer they got to the intersection, the busier it looked. Volunteers loaded injured people into the backs of pickup trucks, carried them in their arms, or helped them hobble into the vehicles. The bright blue lights of police cars lit up the neighborhood.

"I want to talk to an officer," Pierre said, tugging her toward a policeman.

The officer was speaking into his radio when they approached. He reattached the radio to his vest and looked at Pierre. "How can I help you?"

"How bad is it?" Pierre asked. "Was it just our street?"

The officer exhaled. "No. The tornado took out a huge chunk of the downtown area as well, and everything in between."

Penny's mind flashed to her aging mother, helpless in the assisted living center. "What about the north side of town?"

He shook his head. "No damage there. Maybe some strong winds, but nothing too threatening."

Penny closed her eyes. Praise the Lord. She turned to Pierre. "Your daughter's safe, too, then. They were shopping on the west side."

"Thank you, officer." Pierre turned to Penny. "Let's go to Linda's house then," he said, referring to his ex-wife. "They probably went home after shopping."

It would take at least an hour to walk down Range Line and get to the house, but at least it was a plan. It was better than worrying about her son and his Domino's deliveries.

Range Line lay in ruins. Penny tried not to gasp or cry out as they walked past what should've been familiar landmarks. Everything was gone. The streets were crowded with people, some crying, others running from one place to another, and some sitting on the curb with shocked expressions on their faces.

"Do you need help?" a young man asked Pierre. "Are you okay?"

Pierre gave a sharp wave. "We're fine."

"Thanks for asking," Penny added, touched that with all the devastation, someone actually took time to notice them and care for their welfare.

Downed utility lines sparked on the sidewalks, and Pierre wrapped an arm around Penny's waist, giving a wide berth around any dangers. Someone offered them a bottle of water, which he accepted.

"Honey," he said, taking a swig before handing her the bottle, "they're looking at us like we're homeless."

Penny looked up at Pierre, taking in his rugged features and concerned expression. "We really are, dear."

Pierre met her eyes and let out a deep laugh. Penny couldn't help joining him.

They encountered a police blockade at the next street. "You can't go past this point," the officer in a bright orange vest said. "There are too many power lines down. We're working on getting the power off, but it's not safe."

"That's fine. We'll go this way." Pierre turned Penny down another street.

"I need a break, Pierre," Penny said, hating to admit the exhaustion she felt. The cold seeped into her bones, permeating her still-wet clothing.

"Let's sit for a bit." Pierre seated himself at the curb, pulling her down next to him.

Penny leaned on his shoulder and took several deep breaths, trying to keep the anxiety and fear at bay. "I want to talk to my mom. I need to let her know we're okay." She opened her phone again. Still nothing.

"Ma'am?" A woman in her mid-thirties leaned over them. "Would you like a towel?" She held out a thick, maroon-colored towel toward Penny.

"Yes," Penny said. She clutched the soft material against her shivering body. "Thank you."

"And for you, sir." The woman gave one to Pierre with a small smile, then she ducked her head and hurried away, a bundle of towels in her arms.

Again tears burned Penny's eyes, and she blinked them back. "I'm ready."

Pierre got to his feet with a grunt. "All right. Let's go." He walked slower now, and Penny noticed the way he favored his cut leg. How bad was it? Would he need surgery? What if it got infected?

Never mind that now. She'd go crazy if she thought of these things. They just had to get to Linda's house, then they'd worry.

Chapter Ten

Late Sunday night, May 22, 2011
Approximately 5 hours after tornado strike

"My cell phone would not work. I felt stranded. I didn't know who was where. I didn't know what was going on." – Tommie K. Ava

Cara Edens' Home

Cara spent the next half hour working with her family members, trying to salvage everything they could.

"We have to worry about looters," Mr. Edens said. "Put everything you think can be saved in Uncle Todd's truck."

Cara found a soiled shirt and one soaked shoe. Clothes and shoes could be washed. She glanced at her family members. They were still in their comfy clothes, more suitable for watching Sunday sports than cleaning up wreckage. Her nephew was wrapped in his grandfather's hoodie. His overnight bag was missing, so they'd stripped him of his wet clothes. By some miracle, Cara's mom had found a clean diaper. Now he huddled next to Cara's dad.

"Mom." Julie stepped over broken boards, her fiance Sam by her side. "I haven't seen my house yet. Can we leave Caleb with you?"

Mrs. Edens pushed back a strand of short brown hair. "Of course. He's fine with your dad, anyway."

Julie gave her a smile. "Thanks."

"Do you need help?" Cara asked. Her sister only lived six blocks away, and Cara knew there was a good chance that their house had been destroyed, too.

Julie's smile wavered. "I'll let you know."

"Fair enough." Cara gave her a quick hug.

Julie and Sam went with Uncle Todd to the truck, and he drove them away.

Darkness descended, and they had to stop working. Cara held Caleb in her arms and clutched Stephen's hand. She could smell the natural gas leak from St. John's, not too far from them. They sat on the curb and waited for Uncle Todd. Exhaustion pounded in her temples and her eyes burned, though that might have been from the constant stream of tears while she worked.

Uncle Todd returned without Julie and Sam. "Julie's house was destroyed also. They're looking for a few things," he said to Cara. "I'll take everyone to my house. You have a place to stay?"

She nodded. "Yes." She handed over Caleb. "Stephen's car's not too far."

"Be careful," her father said, giving her a hug.

"Actually," Stephen said, "Could we get a lift to the car? It's dark. We won't be able to see what we're walking on."

"Of course." Uncle Todd nodded. "Climb on in."

It took over an hour to drive from the south of town to Schifferdecker. From there they had to back track to 20th Street, and then to Connor. There were fewer people out, but lots of debris. They made slow progress getting back to their car. The gas leak by St. John's forced them to detour.

Uncle Todd's small truck had four seats, but there wasn't room for all the adults. Stephen and her dad sat in the bed of the truck. Cara kept glancing back at them, worried a tornado might appear out of thin air and snatch them up.

Julie called, and Cara gave her directions to Stephen's car. She and Sam planned to meet them there.

The minutes crept by and Uncle Todd's truck barely moved. Cara's eyes darted to the clock on the dash and she sighed. "We could have walked the distance by now." She didn't mean to sound grouchy, but she was tired. Wouldn't they ever get there?

Julie and Sam were waiting at the car when they arrived.

"Our house is gone," Julie said, her lip quivering. "Sam wants to go to his parents' in Webb City. I want to stay here."

Cara gave her a big hug. "We'll help however we can."

Julie glanced at her fiancé. "There are a few things back at the house we want to go back and get. Can you drive us there?"

"Sure." Stephen opened the door to the car. "Climb in."

Cara checked her phone as soon as she got in the car. Dozens of friends had texted or called, including Stephen's mom. He called her back while Julie and Sam climbed into the car. Nothing from her friend Emily, though. Cara tried to reach her, but the call didn't go through.

The McMinn Family

Kayla's father drove her, Justin, and the kids to Kayla's sister's house in Miami, Oklahoma to spend the night. Kayla had her purse on one shoulder. Next to her purse sat the PlayStation she'd saved from the house.

"We never did find Brad," she said to Justin, referencing the memory box.

He squeezed her neck. "We'll find him."

Her father stuck around long enough for all the kids to get into the house. "I have to go to work," he said. "I'm on the night shift rotation."

Kayla nodded. She knew what life with a cop was like. Her dad had been one for twenty-three years. "Thanks for all your help tonight, Dad."

Kayla's sister Sara brought in the children, then set them up in the den. Kayla helped Sara set out blankets and pillows all over the floor to sleep on. There wasn't a lot of room in the small house; it barely fit Sara's family, and definitely didn't fit Kayla's.

"What's this?" Kayla picked at a black spot on Clark's ear. Her finger came away with dirt on it. She checked his other ear. Dirt caked both of his lobes all the way to the ear canal. "Oh no. We have to wash some ears."

The boys cried, but Kayla made them sit in the bathroom while she cleaned the dirt from their ears. Then she had to do it to her own ears, as dirt and debris kept falling out. "You too, Justin!" she hollered. "Clean your ears!"

Once everyone had been washed and cleaned, Kayla lay the kids down. In spite of the events of the day, they fell right to sleep.

Not Kayla. She spent the first hour trying to activate her phone with her new card. All the lines in Joplin seemed to be busy, and she couldn't get through to the activation line. She finally got it activated and called friends and family to let them know she was okay. Those who didn't answer she tried over and over again, worrying as the hours crept by. She kept thinking about Stephanie and Donny. Guilt plagued her for not getting out of the bathtub sooner. Maybe she would've been able to help find them, but she couldn't have left her babies in there by themselves. She tried calling Stephanie again, getting the same response. It just rang and rang.

The Scaggs Household

Meg's father took her and the kids to his house. Her parents had recently moved, which was incredibly fortunate. The old house, which they had been trying to rent to tenants, was destroyed in the tornado. Luckily it was vacant.

Meg sat in the living room of her parents' house while her dad poured a shot of whisky for her. Meg took the glass and clasped her father's hand.

"I'm just so glad you're okay," Meg whispered. "You and Eileen. I couldn't bear it if something happened to you."

"We are all blessed."

Meg stared into her glass. This was her second shot, but it wasn't making her feel any better. She'd been trying to call friends and coworkers all evening, with no response. Were they as blessed? "Have you talked to Mom?"

"Yes, I finally got a call out. She's catching a flight back from Florida tomorrow morning. Any word from Scott?"

Meg shook her head. "He might not have very good cell service either. I'm sure he's fine." But of course she wasn't sure. How could she be? She just had to trust that Scott would be safe. He was helping people. Nothing bad would happen. She downed her drink, then stood and poured herself another. "How far did this tornado go? How many people did it affect?"

"I have no idea, Meg. None of our cell phones are working, either."

"But your Internet is." Meg stood up, suddenly having an idea. "Can I use your computer?" If people had Internet access, she could bet that Facebook would have updated information.

Meg logged into her account. The first thing she noticed was a status update from Scott's account that included Meg in it. *He must've been able to post from his phone*, she thought.

"My family and I are okay. Our house is gone, but we are okay."

The Jason Residence

The stars were out by the time they reached Linda's house. Pierre rang the doorbell and leaned against a pillar on the porch. Penny's legs gave out and she sank onto the steps.

Pierre's daughter opened the door. "Hey!" Tara said with a smile. "What are you guys doing here?"

Her countenance was all wrong. Penny peered up at her and frowned. How could she act so light and frivolous after such a tragedy?

Pierre wrapped her up in a big hug. "I'm so glad you're all right, honey."

She laughed and shied away from her father, a note of

141

apprehension appearing in her eyes. "What do you mean? Of course I'm fine."

"We lost the house," Penny burst out, unable to bear Tara's happy ignorance any longer. "We managed to get out of the rubble."

Tara's smile dimmed but stayed where it was. "What do you mean, Penny?" Her eyes flicked to Pierre's. "How could you lose a house?"

Linda's footsteps pounded across the hardwood floor, and she appeared in the doorway behind Tara. "Penny. Pierre. Come in."

Finally, Penny thought, trying to feel gracious toward her husband's ex.

"Mom?" Tara said as Linda shut the door. "What's Dad talking about? Losing a house?"

Linda sighed and ran a hand through her wavy auburn hair. "I didn't want to worry her, Pierre. Especially when neither you nor Penny answered your cell phones."

"Worry me?" Tara's voice rose in pitch rapidly as only a dramatic teenager's can. "You mean the house is really gone? What? How?"

"Tornado, honey," Pierre said, taking her shoulders in his hands. "The whole house is gone."

"My room. My things." Tara's eyes welled up. She blinked and forced a smile as tears rolled down her face. "But you're okay? You got out?"

"We made it," Penny agreed. Her eyes were riveted to Pierre's leg, where, for the first time, she noticed a crimson stain seeping through his sweatpants. "But not unscathed. Sit down, Pierre."

He started to protest, but Penny gave him her best no-nonsense look. Hanging his head, he lowered himself onto the sofa.

Penny started to roll up his pant leg but stopped when he groaned. Besides that, she could tell from the blood dripping down his shin that it was bad. "Linda? I need some help here."

142

Linda knelt next to Penny and crinkled her nose at the sight. "Hang on." As a former nurse, Linda had a lot of experience caring for and bandaging wounds.

It took her all of ten minutes to disinfect the wound and stop the bleeding. "Any other injuries?"

"No." Penny shook her head, overwhelmed again with gratitude. "Somehow we're okay, praise the Lord."

"Well, what can I do for you right now? Need a place to sleep? Food? You're welcome to whatever I have."

Penny hesitated. She appreciated all Linda was offering, but what she really wanted... "Actually, do you have a car we can use? I'd really like to check on my son."

Linda snapped her fingers. "I've got just the thing. Come on."

Inside the garage, Linda led them to a beat-up white pickup truck. "It still runs. I just don't need it."

"Thank you, thank you, thank you!" Penny said, throwing her arms around Linda. "I've got to go. Pierre, I've got to go."

"I'm coming too." Pierre had already pulled himself into the passenger side. "You think I'd let you go alone in this?"

"I'm driving," Linda said. "Everyone pile in."

She started the truck and backed down the driveway. Squished between Tara and Pierre, Penny watched the road, glad no people or vehicles milled about this far north. Taking backroads and detours to avoid traffic and congestion, it took nearly thirty minutes to get to Domino's. Penny scanned the parking lot and didn't see her son's car.

Pierre squeezed her hand. "Take a deep breath, Pen. Let's go in."

Right. Penny took several breaths, preparing herself for whatever they might hear.

"We'll stay here," Linda said, taking her daughter's hand.

Penny nodded.

No one was making pizza. The store wasn't closed, but the employees stood huddled around the cash register, their voices a low murmur in the quiet restaurant.

"Penny!" Brad, the manager, called when he saw her. He came around the counter and shook her arm. "Are you looking for Josh? He's not here. Boy, am I glad to see you!"

"Why?" Penny asked, swallowing hard in her dry mouth. "Where is he?"

"Looking for you, of course!"

"He's okay?" she breathed, her legs almost giving out beneath her. Pierre braced her shoulders and held her up.

"Yes, he's fine." The manager practically beamed. "He was doing a delivery out on the state line. We couldn't reach him on his phone and didn't know he was okay until he got back." Brad chuckled. "Turned out he didn't even know about the tornado! We started crying and hugging him and he was like, 'What? Get off me!'"

Penny pressed a hand to her heart, unable to keep the tears at bay. They'd found Tara, and Josh was all right. Was it possible her family had made it through this?

Brad's expression sobered. "We all drove out to your house when we heard what side of town the tornado hit. When Josh saw the wreckage, he thought you were in it. He ran out of the car and started searching for you. He told us to check on our families, that he'd keep working there. So we did. When we tried to go back, the road was closed."

"Thank you." Penny turned around, her head clear again. "We've got to get back to the house, Pierre."

The Borup Family

It took almost two hours to get to Hannah's house. They had to park the car and start walking. The air was beginning to feel chilly, even though it was May.

Jessica broke into tears when they left the car. She walked with her head down, sobbing as they passed through debris and scattered belongings.

The sight of everything, coupled with Jessica's outburst, brought a lump to Melinda's throat. She worked hard to get her emotions under control. She couldn't let herself be overwhelmed by this. Instead, she tried to make light of it. "It's the flip-flops, isn't it? They hurt your feet."

Jessica gave a halfhearted smile. "Yeah. I didn't think we'd be doing all this walking." Then her smile wobbled, and she burst into tears again.

Melinda forced herself to look straight ahead. Bloodied and battered people were everywhere, most of them being helped. Some were just being moved. She put on her tunnel vision and focused on getting to Hannah's house. She spotted a board with nails in it and turned to Jessica. "Watch your step, okay?"

Jessica nodded, tears still trailing down her face. She swept her eyes from one side of the road to the other, and Melinda knew she was taking it all in.

At one point the debris in the road was so bad, they couldn't keep walking. Melinda led Jessica into the muddy grass, but she worried about what her daughter might step on.

Hannah lived nine blocks from Walmart. All the people and the hazardous debris made the walk even slower than usual. When they reached Hannah's house, they found Hannah, her brother, her parents, and her grandparents sitting behind the house by the storm shelter. They were wet from the rain that poured down on them, and Melinda imagined they were cold, also. Jessica ran to her friend and the two of them hugged and cried together.

"It's a long walk back," Melinda said, helping the other family members to their feet. "We better get started."

"We have an opening here." Hannah's mom moved a few boards away from the demolished house. "There might be some things we need to take."

"Like what?" her husband asked.

Melinda tapped her teeth together. "It's getting dark, and the road is dangerous. We need to leave."

"Just one more thing," Hannah's grandma said, stumbling toward the wreckage of the house. Melinda noticed she had a plastic Walmart bag on each arm. "I need to check for something."

"Not you, Mom. Stay here. I'll be quick." Hannah's mom disappeared, then came out with a few things in her hands.

"Is that it, then?" Melinda asked, impatient to get going.

"I need to check something," Hannah's grandma said again, pushing toward the house.

"Mom!" Hannah's mom jumped up and grabbed the old lady's shoulders. "Not again. Melinda's right. We have to leave before it gets dark." She met Melinda's eyes and mouthed a "sorry" as they headed for the street. They started walking, and she leaned in and whispered, "We've had the hardest time getting her to leave the house. We practically had to drag her."

Melinda nodded. "It's just really bad out here. You have no idea."

"Well, I have some," she said. "Dan went out to see what things were like. He told us about it."

"Oh, good," Melinda said, trying to keep the sarcasm from her voice. "Then there won't be any surprises."

They walked along the street and sidewalk, past a downed cell tower. Melinda examined it as they passed. The tornado had plucked it up, twisted it, turned it over, and dropped it. The power of the wind astonished her.

Every hundred feet, Hannah's grandmother stooped to the ground, picked something up, and dropped it into one of her Walmart bags. Melinda stepped back to see if she could help her. Her mouth fell open as she realized what was happening: the Walmart bags had holes in them, and every few feet the old woman's "valuables" would fall out. What floored Melinda were the items she considered valuable: batteries and coins.

It was so crazy that Melinda almost laughed. The old lady hadn't thought to grab a coat, or gloves, or anything useful. But batteries and coins were suddenly treasures.

It continued to sprinkle. The water, combined with the wind, made it quite cold, making her wish she had a coat.

They came upon a pasture, and Hannah's brother stopped. "Dad," he asked, "where are all the cows?"

Melinda looked at the field too. She hadn't even thought about the animals. But where had they gone? Where was the livestock?

As they neared the car, Melinda saw fire department personnel going from house to house, spray-painting orange Xs on homes. They wrapped the porches of some in yellow caution tape. Melinda smelled natural gas all around them, and sometimes they had to walk around gas spraying out of the dirt.

"Look at that house," Hannah said, pointing to a large gray house in the middle of the destruction that had somehow come away unscathed. "How did those people get so lucky?"

Melinda stared at them. What surprised her was not that their house was okay, but that instead of helping, giving out water or some other aid, they sat in rocking chairs on the porch, beer bottles in their hands.

The Mitchells

The paramedics hurried Nellie, James, and her mother out of the ambulance and to the triage unit. Nellie watched doctors and nurses evacuate the hospital, which looked like it had been bombed.

Her mother whimpered, and Nellie whirled around. For the first time, she had an expression on her face: fear. Her wide eyes flickered around the scene, and her arms trembled around her dog.

"She's in shock," Nellie heard another man say. "We need to move her to another hospital."

Nellie grabbed the man's arm as he hurried by. "Which hospital are you taking her to?"

"I don't know." He shook her off. "Depends which ambulance we put her in." He didn't give her a chance to ask more questions before he rushed to another injured person.

Nellie picked up her mom's purse and sifted through it, looking for some sort of identification that would help them contact Nellie. She found a picture of her and her brother. She flipped it over and wrote her phone number on it, then put it back in the purse.

The paramedics laid her mother on a stretcher and handed the dog to Nellie.

"Can I go with her?" Nellie asked, putting the purse in the crook of her mother's arm.

"Sorry, ma'am," the paramedic said. "We're already cramming four to five people in an ambulance. There's no room. I won't even know which ambulance I'm putting her in until we get through the line."

"You don't know where she's going?"

"No, ma'am. But I know she'll be undergoing surgery, and soon."

Nellie had suspected as much. Still, it was disheartening. She leaned closer to her mother. "Mom, call me. Wherever they take you, call me." She fought back the crazy feeling that she would lose her mother, never see her again. She hated not knowing where she was going.

Nellie watched them put her into an ambulance and drive away. She and James walked all the way back to their house with Nellie's mom's fat little dog in their arms. Nellie's cell phone rang as they walked. It was a Joplin number, so Nellie answered. "Hello?"

"Is this Nellie Mitchell?" A formal female voice asked.

"It is," Nellie replied.

"I'm calling in regards to your mother."

Nellie's heart rate quickened, but she kept silent.

"She's here at the temporary surgical center. We have a surgeon available. He cleaned her wound and stitched it up, and it doesn't look like she'll need surgery. We'll call you when she's ready to go home."

"Thank you," Nellie said. "I'll wait for the phone call."

"What was that?" James asked.

148

"My mom's okay. They already stitched up her leg. We can get her soon."

"That's great," he said. "Where is she?"

"She's..." Nellie trailed off. If the woman had said where her mom was, Nellie couldn't remember. "Let me call her back." She dialed the number on her cell phone, but all she got was a busy signal. "I don't know. I'll have to wait until they call again."

The house still didn't have electricity, so James took her to his sister's house.

"I hate to intrude on them," Nellie said as they pulled up. "Isn't it your niece's birthday today?"

"Yeah," James said. "I'm sure she'll never forget today. Don't worry, they'll be happy to help us out. Then I have to leave and see if the hospital needs assistance." He glanced at Nellie as if waiting for her reaction, but she only nodded.

Nellie knew he had recently conducted a drill at the hospital for a natural disaster. Now the real thing had happened, and he needed to be onsite to see how it had played out. As the safety officer, it was his job to assist and oversee hospital operations in case of an emergency. Nellie had the feeling he'd be working more than his usual nine-to-five for a while.

The Divine Household

Piper finally got to her own house. Everything looked fine. Rain fell on the entire neighborhood, but as far as she could tell, none of the homes had any damage. Relieved, Piper headed for her mom's apartment a few blocks away.

Her phone dinged. She checked it, surprised to see a text, and from her mom at that.

"Where R U? U OK?"

Piper quickly texted back, "Took detour. Bad traffic. On my way. U OK?"

"OK. No damage. Be careful."

Traffic on 7th Street was still incredibly backed up.

Police had set up patrols on both sides of the damage zone. Electronic noises from the backseat indicated that Michael had set down his book and picked up his DS.

Piper pulled up in front of her mother's apartment.

"Hey," Michael said, undoing his seatbelt. "We're at Nana's house. Great, I'm starving."

Piper's mom came out of the front door before Piper had even shut the car off. Piper raced up the steps and threw her arms around her mom. All of the sudden, the tears started coming, and Piper couldn't stop them. She bawled, remembering everything she'd seen.

"Oh, honey, it's okay," her mom whispered, rubbing her back.

"It was awful," Piper sobbed. "So awful."

"I know. I've been watching the news. I went out too. I tried to check on your cousins who live by the high school. I got as far as 15th Street and I couldn't go any farther. It's horrible. But we're all right. We made it."

"You're apartment's okay?" Piper wiped her eyes and looked around. Several of the neighboring apartments were missing sections of shingles or had windows blown out.

"I'm fine. I even have electricity. We got lucky."

"I was so worried when I couldn't reach you."

"Phone's aren't working right," her mom said.

"Yeah." Piper sent off a text. "I figured. I haven't been able to get people to answer." She pulled up Facebook and scrolled through statuses. It seemed to be the most reliable way to reach people right now.

Chapter Eleven

Around Midnight, May 22, 2011
Approximately 7 hours after tornado strike

"We had no ID...we had nothing but the drenched and dirty clothes we had on." — *Diane Humphrey*

The Divine Household

Piper wished she could stay at her mom's, but she left, arriving at her house around ten-thirty. She turned the radio on, listening for updates. "Get ready for bed, Michael," she told her son. "It's late."

"Yeah." He finally put his book down and went to his room.

Piper did a few random housecleaning tasks, mostly to take her mind off the sights she'd seen. She tried again to call Ashley, her newly married friend, but the call still didn't go through. She tried not to worry, even though she knew Ashley had been on the destroyed side of town, shopping, earlier in the day. She just hoped she'd gotten home in time.

And what about her husband? As a fireman, he must be out there, putting himself in danger to help people. Piper wished she could reach her.

"I just got a printed bulletin. This is an important announcement for families in Joplin." The newscaster's voice became official.

Piper turned toward the radio, listening.

"School has been closed for the remainder of the year."

"Does that mean I don't have to go to bed?" Michael appeared in the kitchen doorway.

"You still need to go to bed," Piper said, though in reality she didn't care. "But you can read for a bit more if you want."

She lay down and tried to sleep, but her mind wouldn't stop replaying the scenes from the drive home, especially of the dead women. Her heart pounded every time she remembered them, and she felt guilty for not doing something to help them. But how could she help? They were dead. She tried to reason with herself, but the overwhelming feeling that she didn't deserve to be sleeping in a warm, intact house while others suffered wouldn't leave her alone.

The Borup Family

They were an hour away from Hannah's house when Melinda realized the debris between Range Line and 22nd would be too much for her to drive through, and that was the route she needed to take to pick up Richard. She tried calling him, but only got a busy signal.

Melinda paused a moment to send him a text. "Bad debris. Cant get thru. Come to car."

It took several minutes, but Richard responded. "Going to restaurant. Pick us up."

Melinda texted back, "OK."

Walking back to the car was exhausting. The group trudged forward in silence, every ounce of energy going into putting one foot in front of the other. About half a mile from the car, a van stopped.

"Where are you going?" the driver, a tired, nice-looking man with a beard asked.

"Just a half mile more," Melinda said. "My car's up there."

"We have room for two more. We'll give some of you a ride."

"Take my parents." Hannah's mom stepped forward, guiding her parents to the van. "This journey's been hard

152

on us."

Melinda described the car, telling him it was in the Walmart parking lot. The van drove off with the older couple, and the rest of them continued on.

The grandparents were waiting when they arrived at the car, and Melinda piled the two families inside. Fire trucks and ambulances poured out of the St. Freeman's parking lot, making it difficult to turn left. Melinda just wanted to get home. She felt on the verge of tears, and she could not cry here, not now. She glanced at the cars jockeying for position around her. Some of them were so damaged that she couldn't believe they were drivable. She pointed out a fender bender.

"Any guesses?" she asked. "Was that a deer before the tornado, or a tree after the tornado?"

Hannah's mom snorted, and then began to laugh. "The question is, will the insurance company know the difference?"

Melinda laughed too. She welcomed the humor, as it took her mind off crying. Her stomach rumbled, and Melinda realized she hadn't eaten since before church. She imagined everyone else was just as hungry. She searched for an open fast-food joint as they drove, finally spotting a Schlotzky's that appeared to be fully functioning.

When they finally got home Melinda was beyond exhausted. But she still had to get back out there and find Richard and the Wrights.

She threw open the hall closet and tossed out blankets. "Jessica, help Hannah and her family find places to sleep. I'll be back."

"Sure, Mom." Jessica took over and Melinda left.

She drove the car back into the destruction, trying to get to the restaurant Richard had told her to meet him at. It had been four hours since he'd left running for their house. Melinda wouldn't let herself worry.

People walked on either side of her, sometimes moving faster than her car. Melinda looked out the driver's side and saw an elderly man and woman walking in the street. Rather, he was walking and pushing her in a wheelchair. The road started to incline, and he slowed, taking wobbly steps as he pushed her. The rain made the road slicker than usual, and she could see how he struggled.

I should offer them a ride, Melinda thought.

Traffic moved again and she inched past them. *No, I can't. I'm trying to get to Richard.* She drove past the couple and pushed down the urge to help them.

When she finally got to the restaurant, she breathed a sigh of relief. There was Richard with the Wrights, a stroller full of bags and belongings between them. Richard carried their baby in his arms.

"The Bartows called someone else," he said.

"And we just got a hold of my sister," Mrs. Wright said. "She'll be here soon."

"Yeah," Richard said. "I'm just waiting until she gets here."

Mr. Wright put a hand on Richard's shoulder. "He helped a lot. He carried the baby the whole way here."

Melinda hugged Richard. "Good job, Richard," she whispered, giving him a quick squeeze. She waited with him until Mrs. Wright's sister arrived.

Her thoughts returned to that couple she'd seen pushing up the road, and she felt a flash of guilt. She could've stopped, and she should have.

When she and Richard finally got home, Melinda did a quick headcount. Of course, all of her family was here. They also had Hannah's family. And then the neighbor's family had come over because they didn't have a tornado shelter and were afraid to stay in their house, in case another storm came.

There was no electricity either, so candles and flashlights sporadically lit the halls and rooms. Melinda lost count at around eighteen people and four dogs. She spent the evening pulling down blankets and pillows, trying to situate all the families in comfortable rooms. Once again, she was very grateful that her family had two washers and dryers.

When Melinda finally lay down, she was utterly exhausted. She closed her eyes, willing sleep to come. But it didn't. All evening she'd heard those around her talk about the noise, how loud the tornado was. Her friend's husband was a policeman, and he kept talking about how he couldn't get the sound out of his head.

Melinda couldn't remember hearing it. What she remembered was seeing it. Even now she could see the way the world spun when the tornado surrounded them. She swallowed against a dizzy, nauseous feeling and gripped the side of the bed, overwhelmed by a sense of vertigo.

Sleep never did come.

The McMinn Family

Kayla paced the kitchen floor, dialing the same numbers over and over. It was a little after two a.m. when Kayla's friend Stephanie finally answered the phone.

"Hello?" she greeted in a voice drunk with exhaustion.

"Thank goodness," Kayla breathed. "I was so worried! I've been calling for hours!"

"Kayla, are you all right?" Stephanie asked. "All I could think about was you and those babies. I just knew something was wrong. I saw your house. It's gone."

"Just like yours," Kayla confirmed, not about to accept sympathy from a fellow victim. "We're fine. Just bumps and bruises. But where were you? I kept calling."

"Yeah, I haven't had really good phone service." Stephanie sighed. "I've been at the hospital."

Kayla swallowed hard. She wouldn't be able to handle any more death. "Is everything okay?" she asked tentatively.

"Yeah, yeah, we're fine," Stephanie said, and Kayla breathed a sigh of relief. "We got lucky. We were blown out of the house when the first part of the storm came through. Then we ran. We hid in the big ditch, you know, the one under the tiny bridge?"

Kayla nodded, knowing which one Stephanie meant. Most people didn't even know the bridge was there. It was small and easy to miss.

"Anyway," Stephanie went on, not waiting for a response, "we got under it, just as the second part of the storm came through. I guess we got away during the eye of the storm? Hank and I both had horrible cuts on our heads, but we've been stitched up. After it was over, we saw a guy with a truck. We flagged him down and he gave us a ride to the hospital. We saw your house as we went by, saw that it was gone. Donny, though," her voice cracked for a moment at the mention of their three-year-old son. "We thought we'd have to cut off his big toe. His foot was pretty bad, but the doctors saved it."

"That's great," Kayla said, because she didn't know what else to say. She felt overwhelmed by emotion, and couldn't quite pinpoint why. "Stephanie, I'm so glad you're fine. I'm going to go to bed now, but call me if anything happens."

"I will. Thanks, Kayla."

Kayla put the phone down and sank into a hard kitchen chair. *Oh my dear Lord,* she thought. *We almost died today. My babies almost died.* The memory of the tornado pulling on the mattress, pulling at the two small children in her arms, cut through Kayla like a shard of glass. She put her head in her hands and sobbed.

Justin found her there and pulled her down to the mattress he'd laid out on the floor for them. He settled behind her and enfolded her in his arms. "I saw the worst things," he whispered. "There was a little boy stuck under a light post. I picked up the post while his mom pulled him out. Kayla." Justin pressed his head into the back of her shoulder, as if to purge the memory from his head. "Half of his body was crushed."

"We were so lucky," Kayla whispered back, unable to wrap her mind around such horrors.

Cara Edens' Home

Cara's parents were still in Uncle Todd's car. "I'll take them to my house," he said to Stephen through the window. "Bring Julie and Caleb over when you're done."

"You got it," Stephen said. He pulled away from the curb and started down the street.

Julie and Sam found a few important items in the wreckage of the house, but by then the rain and darkness made it impossible to keep searching.

"We'll come back tomorrow, Julie," Cara promised, trying to make her feel better.

Julie sniffed, wiping at tears as they rolled down her face. "I hate to ask one more thing. Can you give Sam a ride to his dad's house?"

"You don't even have to ask."

Caleb slept in the car the whole drive to Webb City.

"I need gas," Stephen said after he dropped Sam off. He pulled over to an untouched gas station in front of Walmart.

"And we need food," Cara said, her stomach clenching at the very thought. She glanced at Julie and her sister nodded in agreement.

Stephen pointed out the window. "Speak and your wish is granted. Sonic's open."

"Still?" Cara raised her head in surprise. Cara usually only hit Sonic up during happy hour for the half-off drinks, but she knew it closed at eleven on Sundays. It was after two in the morning, yet dozens of cars were parked around the fast-food restaurant.

"Must be open late because of the tornado," Stephen said. He finished filling up and pulled into the restaurant.

They had to wait in line for cars to get their orders and leave before they got a spot. Cara's body ached with anticipation of a big juicy burger.

Stephen rolled down the window. "Twenty-five burgers, please." He smiled at Cara. "That should feed everyone, right?"

157

TORNADO WARNING

After dropping Julie and Caleb off at Uncle Todd's house, Stephen and Cara finally pulled into their own apartment building. Cara stumbled up the stairs. She pulled the mattress off the bed and laid it on the floor. Somehow, being closer to the ground felt safer. Stephen lay down on it.

Now that it was quiet, sleep wouldn't come. Cara kept picturing her parents' house, the destroyed lot, what might have happened if her father hadn't made it into the closet. Tears continually leaked from the corners of her eyes, and she tried not to make a sound.

"It'll be okay, Cara," Stephen said, as if knowing what she felt.

"I know," she whimpered, pressing her hands to her mouth.

They whispered together for a bit, then fell silent. Cara got up and turned on the radio on the nightstand. A DJ spoke, still live despite the early morning hour.

"We're still taking calls," he said. "All night long, as long as you have something to say. Call us. Tell us what happened today. We're also compiling a list of missing people. We're here for you, Joplin. Let us help."

Cara lay back on the mattress and listened to people calling in. She felt connected to them, hearing their experiences. People gave out contact information to friends and family, anyone who might be listening.

One woman called in, panicking because she couldn't find her mom. "She was at St. John's," the woman said. "But they moved her after the tornado came through. Only, there's no paperwork. I don't know if she's in Springfield, St. Louis, or Kansas City!"

Several other people called in with similar stories. Cara closed her eyes. This didn't feel real. What would she find the next day? How many people that she knew had lost their homes? How would her parents recover from this?

The thoughts overwhelmed her. She knew Stephen had fallen asleep when she heard him snoring. He only snored

158

when he slept on his back, and even then only if he was really out. Cara pulled a blanket over her head, wishing she could silence her thoughts and get some sleep.

The Scaggs Household

Meg felt Scott climb into the bed next to her and she lifted her head. She hadn't really been sleeping, anyway. The clock on the nightstand read one a.m. "Scott?" she whispered. "Are you all right?"

He grabbed her and curled his body around hers. "Oh, Meg. All I did today was clear rubble and pull people out of fallen houses. I can't even think anymore."

"It's fine, Scott." Meg's eyes throbbed, even when she closed them. She didn't have any tears left, but she felt awful for Scott. "Just sleep."

The Mitchells

A few of the neighbors were there when Nellie and James walked in to his sister's house. James helped Nellie get settled on the full-sized spare bed in the basement, since there was no extra bedroom upstairs.

"I hate leaving you like this," he said, handing her another blanket.

Even after putting on dry clothes that her sister-in-law lent her, Nellie couldn't shake the chills. She wrapped the blanket around her, pulling it to her chin. "I know. But you have to go to work. They really need you right now."

"Yeah." He kissed her forehead. "See ya."

His sister Jill settled on the end of the bed. "Do you need anything?"

All Nellie really wanted was to sit in a quiet room and watch TV. "Do you mind if I turn the television on?"

"No, of course not." Jill handed her the remote control.

"How was the birthday party?" Though Nellie hardly felt up to small talk, she felt she needed to acknowledge

Jill's situation.

"Fine. She's only three, so we did something small, thank goodness." The doorbell rang, and Jill turned toward the stairs. "I better see who that is. People keep stopping by. I'll be upstairs if you need me."

"Thank you." Nellie turned on the TV and settled against the couch. She tried to lose herself in a sitcom, desperate to pretend the evening hadn't happened. But she couldn't distract herself, no matter how hard she tried. Her mind kept flashing back to the scene at the nursing home, the fire, the cries of the injured.

She sighed and picked up her phone. She needed to call her brother and let him know about their mother.

Her phone wouldn't call out. Nellie tried texting, but the text failed too, giving her a little red "x" on the screen. "Great," she murmured. She knew how much he'd worry, not being able to reach her.

She could access Facebook, though. She began uploading the pictures she'd taken on her phone to her Facebook account.

Once she finished with that, she turned the TV volume down and stared at the set until her eyes glazed over. Her lids grew heavy, and finally she closed them.

Nellie's phone rang, waking her up. She didn't recognize the number but answered it anyway. It took a full minute for the grogginess to clear out of her head enough for her to realize it was a medical center in Galena, Kansas.

Nellie swung her legs over the side of the couch. "You have my mom? Now?"

"Yes. She's ready to discharge. Can you come get her?"

Judging from the urgency in his voice, Nellie knew he meant that there wasn't room for her.

James wasn't back yet. Certainly Jill would let her borrow a car. "Yes. Yes, I'll be right there."

Jill was awake, sitting at the kitchen table with her husband Danny and another man. The other man had a mug of coffee in his hands, his bloodshot eyes moist.

"Jill," Nellie said, pausing in the doorway. "I hate to bug you, but can I borrow your car? I need to go to Kansas and get my mom."

Jill jumped up. "I'll take you. Let's go."

Nellie buckled her seatbelt and waited for Jill to get in. "Thanks so much for the ride."

"Oh, I was happy for the excuse to get away." Jill shook her head. "That man is one of Danny's coworkers. He lost his apartment and everything he had. He's pretty beat up over it."

Nellie nodded. That explained the repressive mood in the room.

Jill lived in the southern part of Joplin, so they took backroads to Galena. Traffic was sparse on this side of town. Nellie rested her head on the window and stared at the blackness outside. In the distance, ambulance sirens pierced the silence.

Rain poured down the entire way to the medical center. Though grateful for Jill's car, Nellie wished James was with her. The rivulets of water on the windshield did little to mask the destruction in the city.

The medical center was fully staffed with plenty of nurses and doctors in scrubs, ready to take on patients. But it looked like most people had already checked out; the center was nearly empty. Though it was almost three in the morning, Nellie's mother was coherent now. She chattered on about the tornado and the damage. Nellie nodded along, her head heavy and numb.

The next obstacle was getting her injured mother down the stairs into Jill's basement.

"I'm so sorry," Jill said, watching Nellie help her down. "I wish I had a room up here."

Nellie's mom had to go down the stairs on all fours. Jill and Nellie helped as much as they could, but all three women were out of breath by the time they reached the last step.

Nellie lowered her mother onto the couch in the large

living area. "Don't worry about a thing," she told Jill. "We're crashing your house."

The front door opened, then slammed shut. Shortly after that, jars jingled as the refrigerator opened.

"Hello?" Jill called.

"Just me." James pounded down the stairs, cheeks flushed from the cold, windy air. "I cleaned out our fridge, so our food's over here now. I'm tired." He didn't wait for a response before throwing himself on top of the bed.

Nellie patted her mom's hand. "Just shout if you need me." She climbed into bed next to James.

The Jason Residence

No matter how Linda tried to get Penny and Pierre close to the remains of their house, they ran into a road blockade. Linda let out a heavy sigh. "I can't get you there." Penny could hear the frustration and weariness in her voice. Linda's generosity was reaching its limits. "Is there somewhere else I can take you? Do you just want to come back to my place?"

Penny didn't, and she knew Linda didn't want them there, either. "No, that's okay, Linda. Take us to my mom's apartment."

"All right," Linda said, turning the truck around.

It took more than an hour to drive across town. The apartment, thank the Lord, was in one piece. Penny thanked Linda and then hurried up to the third floor. Using her key, Penny unlocked the door and stepped inside.

Her mother sat in her comfy chair in the living room portion of the one-room apartment, wringing a washcloth in her hands and staring at the blank television screen. She swiveled when Penny came in.

"Penny!" she cried, and Penny knelt to embrace her. Tears of relief and anguish welled up in Penny's eyes, and she sobbed into her mother's shoulder. Her mother stroked her hair and patted her face.

"It's all right," she soothed. "You're okay. I'm here."

Penny accepted the comfort gladly. The door clicked shut behind Pierre.

"What about the kids?" her mother asked, pulling Penny's face back and meeting her eyes.

"I don't know," Penny blubbered, wiping at her eyes. "Tara's fine, and we think Josh is. I don't know about my grandbabies." All the fear and worry that had been building for hours finally had an outlet, and Penny cried. "I can't reach anyone!"

"The house is gone," Pierre said, still standing and favoring his good leg. "But we're okay."

"You can stay here," Penny's mother said with a firm nod. "I've got room in my place."

Penny tried to make her mother sleep in the twin bed, but her mother insisted that she slept better in her lift chair. Penny turned on the radio and listened to the updates. A little after midnight, her son Josh and his girlfriend showed up. Another tearful reunion ensued.

"Everyone's okay," Josh said. "I've been around to all the houses. Yours is the only one that was destroyed."

Penny uttered a prayer of thanks, knowing how much harder it would've been for any of the families with small children to survive that wreckage.

Josh left around one a.m., and Penny and Pierre climbed into bed. Pierre wrapped his arms around her and held her close.

"I can't believe the house is gone," Penny whispered, tears running down the bridge of her nose. "And Bella. How awful. And that woman's husband, dead."

Pierre rubbed her back and just let her ramble. "But we're still alive," Penny finished. "We're alive. Praise the Lord, we're alive."

Pierre kissed her cheek. "We're alive, Pen. And so are the kids."

"I gotta get to work tomorrow," Penny said, her mind already running through Monday's agenda. "I need to let them know we're okay." She'd worked at Le Barge Electronics for so long, her boss was like a brother.

Pierre squeezed her shoulder. "Worry about it tomorrow."

Penny nodded and let the silence drift over them. She listened to the low murmur of the news on the radio as it gave updates about the tornado damage and rescue operations. Whenever Penny's breathing started to slow, an alarming thought about death tolls and food shortages would send her heart racing again. The constant voice of reassurance finally lulled her into a restless sleep.

Chapter Twelve

Monday, May 23, 2011
Approximately 12 hours after tornado strikes

"Devastation never had a picture in my mind until that day."
— Name Withheld

The McMinn Family

Kayla's mom woke them up at seven a.m. Monday morning. Kayla's head pounded from lack of sleep and the tears she had cried the night before. She let her mom hug her, and she cried some more.

"We need to get back to Joplin," her mom said. "We need to see what's left."

What was left. Kayla put her head in her hands. "We have nothing left. We have no money. We have no cars. How is Justin going to get to work? Is he even going to have a job?" The tears started up again, like a never-ending fountain. "Who's going to need drywall work right now?"

"We'll worry about that later, honey," her mom said. "For now, let's get to Joplin. You might find something important."

Like Brad's memory box.

Kayla didn't know if it had rained all night or just started in the morning, but it was raining as they climbed into her mother's car. The driveway at her sister's house was flooding. Kayla chewed on her nails, already jittery.

Ms. McMinn drove Kayla and Justin back to their house. Kayla had a mental list of all the important items she hoped to find.

When they arrived, however, they found someone had

beat them there: looters.

"The deep freezer's gone!" Justin exploded. "And the stack of electronics I put over here, that I thought I could fix!"

"Here's our stove," Kayla said. Someone had set the stove on top of the rubble. "I guess it was too heavy to steal."

Justin opened it up and peeked inside. "Yeah, but they took our steaks."

Kayla fought the urge to laugh; she'd forgotten about those.

A reporter stood on the corner, snapping photographs of the demolished houses in the neighborhood. Kayla and Justin did their best to ignore the other work parties. Justin had several big cardboard boxes, and they started piling things they could keep into them.

After about an hour, Kayla began to worry. "Justin, I still can't find Brad."

"We'll find him, Kayla," Justin said, nonplussed. "There's a lot of stuff to go through here."

Kayla panicked as the minutes ticked by. A few volunteers joined them, helping them sort through debris. Kayla stopped sorting through items and started thrusting stuff out of the way, clearing a path through the junk.

Still nothing. Kayla burst into tears. "I can't find Brad!"

"Here, calm down." Justin came to her side and gave her a hug. "I'll help you look."

"What's wrong?" one of the volunteers asked, an expression of alarm on his face.

"We can't find Brad!" Kayla said, waving him away. Justin helped her move items to the side and search for the memory box.

"Some help over here!" the volunteer shouted to another party. "We're missing a kid!"

Kayla looked up, her eyes widening. "Oh, no! Not like that! It's his memory box."

"Brad's dead," Justin said, supplying the words that

166

TAMARA HART HEINER

Kayla hated to say.

Kayla sobbed out a laugh. It broke from deep in her chest, and she gave another laugh. Then she cried.

It began to rain harder as the day wore on. Kayla became increasingly more nervous.

"Justin, I want to go," she said. "I think there's another storm coming in."

"Sure, no problem."

Kayla called her mom. "Mom? Come get us. We're done here."

The Jason Residence

Pierre's grunts woke Penny in the morning. She stared at the ceiling for a moment, wondering where she was before memories of last night invaded her mind. She swiveled around to Pierre and grasped his hand. "Honey, are you all right?"

He gave her a squeeze. "Not so great, Pen. But they said on the radio there's a triage set up at Memorial Hall. I need to get there."

He didn't say he needed Penny's help, but she knew that was the only reason he wasn't already there. Penny threw her legs over the side of the bed. Memorial Hall was a block from her mother's apartment. "Come on. Let's take a look at your leg."

A long line crept out the door of the Memorial Hall and down the sidewalk. Penny and Pierre joined it. Some people told stories of their miraculous escapes, but others stood in a quiet, somber silence.

"Penny," Pierre said, breaking the silence, "I don't have any of my meds."

Penny froze. She thought of all the pills in the medicine cabinet upstairs. Without his anti-rejection pills, Pierre's body might suddenly react to the transplanted heart within him. He could only miss three days. She tried to keep her voice calm, though her lip trembled.

"That's all right, I don't have mine either. Maybe they can help us here."

A young man in his early thirties greeted Pierre and Penny when they entered. "Hi, I'm Dr. Southwort. How can I help you?"

Pierre said nothing, so Penny supplied, "He cut his leg yesterday during the tornado. He might need stitches, I'm not sure."

Dr. Southwort nodded. "Let's take a look." He led them to a corner of the front room and sat Pierre in a folding chair. "First I'm going to take your blood pressure and temperature. Then I'll look at your leg. Is it all right if I roll up your pants?"

Pierre cleared his throat. "Yes."

The young man checked Pierre over, then examined his leg. "I don't see any sign of infection, so that's good. But it's a bad enough cut that I want you on antibiotics." He took out his notepad and wrote out a prescription.

"While you're at it," Penny said, trying not to sound too timid, "I lost all my meds in the tornado. Can I get a script for more?" She held her breath, certain he would ask for medical records or doctor numbers.

He didn't even bat an eye. "Of course. Tell me what you were on."

"And Pierre too," Penny let out in a rush. "He needs more meds." She relayed the names and dosages, and the doctor wrote it all down.

"You can fill this prescription at Walmart," he said.

"Thank you," Penny said, taking the paper from him. "I'm sorry, I don't have our insurance cards or my purse..." she trailed off, wondering how she would pay the $200 copay.

He shook his head. "We're not charging for our services right now. If we're going to pull through this, we're going to do it together."

Penny just stared at him. She didn't even know how to thank him for his generosity.

"We appreciate it," Pierre said, standing up and putting an arm around Penny's shoulders. "Thank you." He extended a hand, and the doctor shook it.

"This is why I'm a doctor," he said.

They walked out together, past the long line of those still waiting to be seen. "I guess now we need to get to Walmart," Penny said.

The Walmart on 7th Street was less than two miles from Memorial Hall. They weren't the only ones out on the sidewalk. Rain sprinkled down from the overcast sky, and Penny clung to Pierre, trying to hide behind his larger form. Her clothes had barely dried from yesterday, and here she was getting rained on again.

Another long line greeted them at the pharmacy. The people at the window spoke with angry gestures toward the pharmacists behind it. Penny glanced at the others in line. They all wore similar expressions of defeat and impatience. "What's going on?" she asked the woman in front of her.

Half-turning to face her, the woman said, "The other Walmart's gone. Everyone's here getting prescriptions filled, and they're running out. You won't know if they have yours 'til you get up there."

Great, Penny thought. She sighed and leaned against the toothbrush rack. What could she do to fill the time? They really needed to get back to what was left of the house and see if anything was worth saving. But they didn't have a car, and the thought of walking all that way made her groan out loud.

"It's all right," Pierre said, watching her. "They'll have our meds."

She shook her head. "It's not that. We need a car."

"We should be able to get one," he said. "We had insurance. Why don't you call them?"

Penny straightened and gave a slow nod. "Why didn't I think of that?"

While they waited in line, Penny made several phone

169

calls, first to the insurance company, then to rental car companies. Within minutes, they promised to have a car ready for them to pick up.

She shut her phone and grinned. "Now we just have to walk to the rental place."

Finally it was their turn. It took a lot of discussing and looking for generic substitutions, but she and Pierre were lucky enough to get their meds.

Praise the Lord, Penny thought, her bag of prescription drugs in hand. *It's all working out.* They walked to the rental car company, picked out a car, and drove back to the house.

Penny felt a jolt of shock as they turned the corner. No matter how she prepared herself, she couldn't keep her mouth from dropping at the sight of the destroyed street. Whole trees uprooted, strewn across the sidewalks where workers left them after clearing the road. Houses leveled, leaving nothing but barren plots as far as she could see. "Wow," she breathed.

"Mmm," Pierre grunted, a sound she took as agreement.

"How?" Penny murmured. "How could wind do this?"

Pierre shook his head and parked at the curb next to their house. Up to now, Penny had resisted looking at their own personal devastation. Now she forced herself to turn her head and take it in.

Gone. The house was gone. Tears filled her eyes as she remembered every precious knickknack and memory she'd stored in the building.

Pierre took her left hand and rubbed her fingers. "Let's see if we can find that ring."

The idea of finding her wedding ring in this mess was so ludicrous that Penny laughed. Tears leaked from the corners of her eyes, and she brushed them away. "All right. Let's look."

The rain didn't let up, even though dozens of people stood around their piles of rubble, digging through and looking for things. They only found a few things worth saving before the rain got too hard to keep looking. The wind whipped the bare branches of the few standing trees, and Penny found herself increasingly nervous, glancing over her shoulder and wanting to jump into the car.

"Let's go, Pen," Pierre said, taking her shoulder. "We're done for now."

She couldn't agree more. Nodding, Penny leapt into the rental car and took several deep breaths. *It's just rain*, she told herself. *It's okay.*

Pierre didn't say anything as they drove back to her mom's, and Penny wondered if he had the same anxiety she had. She breathed a deep sigh of relief when they entered the apartment.

"How did it go?" Her mom wheeled over and took Penny's hand.

Penny closed her eyes, picturing again the mass destruction on the whole block. "Mom, it's awful."

"Did you find anything?"

"A few things."

Her mom wheeled around to the low stove. "I made lunch. Just some soup, but it should warm you up."

"Sounds wonderful." Penny and Pierre helped themselves to a bowl. She took a spoonful, blowing on it before placing it in her mouth. "Oh!" she said as the thought just occurred to her, "I haven't called in to work." She turned to Pierre. "I better go. I'll take the rental car."

"You really think you have work today?" He arched a bushy black eyebrow.

"It's a Monday, of course I do. Hopefully I'm not fired." Her work had a zero-tolerance policy on no-shows. Penny gulped down her soup, gave her mom and Pierre a kiss, and headed out the door.

"What are you doing here, Penny?" her boss said when she stepped into the building. "I thought you lived on the south side."

"Well, we do, but..." her voice faltered. She glanced around at the deserted office. "I assumed you would need me."

171

He stepped over to her and put his hands on her shoulders, peering into her eyes. "You and Pierre didn't have any damage?"

She looked down at the beige carpet beneath her mismatched shoes. How ridiculous she must look. "We lost our house."

He exhaled noisily. "You don't need to be here, Penny. Go home. Everyone who's been affected gets time off if needed. That means you, too."

Penny nodded, not able to lift her eyes from her shoes, afraid any compassion in his eyes would bring her to tears. "All right." She had no vacation days left, so the chance to take off and recover from this disaster was a relief, yet at the same time, a disappointment. Work would've helped her focus on something besides herself.

The Divine Household

Piper's mom stopped by her house on Monday morning, waking her up.

"Were you going in to work today?" she asked.

"Yes," Piper said, her voice groggy with exhaustion. "You?" They both worked together at Duke Technology.

"I already went in. They sent me away. Said they don't need us today, that we can take care of things, help people if we want."

Piper nodded, realizing how her mind was not on work anyway. "I'm glad for that. So? What's up?"

"Want to eat breakfast with me?"

The TV and radio warned about the water not being clean enough to drink. Piper rolled out of bed and ran a hand through her short brown hair. "Sounds great."

She got Michael up, and the three of them went to Granny Schaeffer's on 7th Street. Electricity was still spotty in places, so they were glad to find a restaurant that was open.

The place was packed. Piper recognized three or four

people from work, and she nodded at them. She turned to her mom. "Did you tell the boss that I'm okay?"

Her mom shrugged. "I did, of course, but I think they'd rather hear it from you. They asked for everyone to call and give a headcount, let them know if someone can't make it in."

Since they were still waiting to be seated, Piper called her boss. She spoke to him for a few minutes, then hung up. "They're giving everyone today and tomorrow off," she said, still surprised from her conversation. "With pay."

"Oh," her mom breathed. "Isn't that nice?"

"Yeah. He said if we need more time than that, we can ask for an extension." Piper was fine and knew she wouldn't need an extension. But it was a nice gesture, and she felt proud to work with an organization that helped its employees that way.

After breakfast, she went back to her mom's house. She tried to take it easy, to get her body to relax after yesterday's trauma, but she couldn't stop the nervous energy that ran through her. She watched TV for awhile, then took her son and went back home.

Piper still couldn't reach Ashley, and her fear for her friend escalated with every passing hour. She vacillated between feeling totally listless, just sitting in front of the computer and playing games, to going on a productive frenzy, doing laundry and cleaning, the normal things that she would do on a day off. Fortunately for Piper, they never lost electricity. Her gas was off, which was a major inconvenience, and she couldn't use the water, which definitely caused some headaches. Only cold water until the gas came back on, so no shower. But at least she had a house.

The Borup Family

Melinda's family lived on the Freeman grid, which was attached to the Freeman Hospital just over the hill.

The good thing about this was that they had electricity within hours. The city issued a warning to boil all water, so Melinda spent the morning boiling and then storing water for everyone. At least there was plenty for showering.

She set out cereal and oatmeal and let their guests help themselves.

Richard found her doing laundry. She recognized the anxious, pinched look around his eyes. He had a mission to fulfill.

"What is it, honey?" Melinda poured in the soap and turned on the washer.

"I was thinking we should go by the chapel," he said. "There might be people there to pick up. Maybe people waiting for help."

Melinda nodded and put the laundry soap away. "Let me change my clothes." She would not leave the house without pants and tennis shoes, not after last night. She also grabbed her camera. It would be good to document everything she saw.

"Where are you going?" David asked when she opened the front door.

"To the church," she said. "Richard wants to see if anyone needs help."

"I'm coming too," her oldest son said. He rose from the sofa and joined his mom and brother.

"They're not letting anyone into Joplin," David said. "I've been watching the news. The roads have been completely shut down."

"Well, if we can't get there, we'll come back."

Melinda drove slowly through town, taking pictures of the devastation as they went. Seeing things through the lens of a camera helped her deal with it. It made the objects seem less personal and more distant.

They arrived at the church parking lot. The chapel was gone.

Melinda felt as though someone had kicked her in the gut. It hadn't occurred to her that the chapel could go. It seemed like a rock, a safe haven. She pulled the camera out and started snapping pictures. *People will want to see this,* she thought.

A few men walked over the wreckage of the building. Her sons bolted out of the car and ran to them. Melinda followed, though less enthusiastically. Rain plastered her hair to her face and dampened her energy.

Something pushed on the bottom of her foot. Melinda paused and lifted her shoe. A nail. She'd stepped on a nail. She picked at it until she got enough to pull it out. Good thing she'd worn thick-soled shoes.

She recognized the bishop and his son talking to her boys.

"The president lost his home," the bishop greeted her.

"Oh, no," Melinda murmured.

"I've been trying to get into the offices, but I can't. I need to get into the credenza. Lots of important documents and papers are in there." The bishop led them over to the only wall still standing. The bathroom and offices attached to it remained intact. The bishop shoved his body against one of the office doors. "It won't go any farther than this. Something's blocking it." The door opened a few inches and then stopped.

"Let me try." Her oldest son, a very tall and slight young man, slid his body through the crack. "I'm in."

A moment later he got the pathway cleared enough to let everyone else in the room. Melinda spotted the wooden credenza in the corner and exhaled. At least it was still intact.

The bishop knelt in front of it and tried every key on his ring, but none opened it.

"I've got to get this paperwork out of here," he said. "The rain will ruin everything soon."

"Who's got the key?" Richard asked.

"Only the president. And I don't know where he is at the moment."

The bishop's son left the room and came back with a red

175

ax. "How about this?"

"Where did you get that?" Richard asked, his eyes bulging.

"By the fire alarm." The boy shrugged, a pleased expression on his face.

"Stand back." The bishop lifted the ax and began hacking at the credenza. "I'm also going to need the hard drives to the computers."

His son disappeared out the door, returning a moment later. "I can't get any of the offices open."

"We won't let that stop us." The bishop placed the papers from the credenza on the desk, then hefted himself on top as well. He grabbed the edge of the wall and pulled himself up, then dropped into the office on the other side.

Melinda pressed her hands to her mouth, shocked. She remembered her camera at her side, and pulled it out, taking more pictures of the ruined building. She paused outside the offices, running her fingers over the paintings on the wall. They hung untouched. Some things were fine and others were completely gone. Melinda put down the camera.

"Bishop. What about looters?" She studied the paintings, hating the idea of someone destroying them after they had withstood the forces of a tornado.

"There's nothing of value here." His voice carried easily through the offices, since there was no roof on the building.

"What about the paintings?"

"Oh."

Melinda's heartbeat quickened, and she blurted out, "Can I take them home?"

"That's a good idea. We'll know where they are that way."

"Boys, help me," Melinda said.

The rain fell harder. They gathered up the paintings as quickly as they could and moved them to Melinda's car. As far as she could tell, none of them were missing. All of them had some sort of damage to them, but it amazed Melinda that they could come out as undamaged as they had.

The boys went back inside the chapel to help the bishop while Melinda arranged the paintings in the backseat. Her cell phone rang, and she pulled it out.

"Melinda?" David said. "Where are you?"

"I'm at the chapel," Melinda said, glancing out the window at the wrecked building. "It's been leveled, David."

"Leave right now. There's another storm coming from the west. They're predicting sixty-five mile-per-hour winds."

Melinda's hands began to tremble, and she forced herself to breathe deeply. "All right. I'll get the boys. We're coming home." She hung up and dialed Richard's phone. It went straight to voicemail—dead. Just then she spotted the bishop and the three boys racing around the side of the remaining wall.

"Come on!" Melinda shouted. "We've got to leave now!"

The boys jumped into the car. Melinda waited long enough to see the bishop and his son get into their car, then she gunned the engine. The rain poured down harder, and hail started to accompany it.

They sat in silence. Melinda tried to be as calm as they were, but she was terrified. She turned onto Indiana Street, then left at the signal. Her thoughts were focused on getting home as quickly as possible. She turned again.

"Mom," her oldest son said, leaning forward, "where are we?"

"We're on—" Melinda began. She looked for a street sign, but they were all gone. She twisted in her seat, searching for a landmark or something familiar, something that would indicate where they were. "I–I don't know."

"Mom, are we lost?" Richard poked his head between the two seats.

"We can't be lost." How could they be lost? This was Joplin. This was home.

The rain pelted harder, so hard that the windshield wipers couldn't keep up.

"We need to get home," her oldest said, rising up in his seat.

Melinda turned down one street and then down another. They all looked the same.

"There, there!" He bounced up and down. "I see the hospital!"

What was left of it, anyway. St. John's had been decimated. Debris littered the street and block around it, and downed power lines hung like spider webs between houses.

Melinda breathed a sigh of relief. Home was just around the corner. She had to drive under one of the power lines, and she felt it scrape the top of the car. Thank goodness all the power was out.

The Scaggs Household

In spite of the lack of sleep and the exhausting day before, Meg woke up at four thirty in the morning. She reached her hand out and touched Scott's back. She left it there a moment, feeling his ribcage rise and fall with each breath.

Light flickered from the computer on the desk in the corner, and Meg realized her father was on it. "Dad?" she murmured, sitting up. "What are you doing?"

"I just got a press conference from the city manager," he murmured, so soft that Meg could barely hear.

Meg pulled a blanket off the bed and spread it on the carpet near her father. Then she lay down on top of it. Her father kept talking, and Meg couldn't believe what she was hearing.

"So many deaths. More than sixty people dead. Hundreds, maybe even thousands, are missing. Homes destroyed."

Meg listened until he had nothing more to say. After her father vacated the computer, Meg climbed into the chair and logged onto Facebook. Tears welled in her eyes as she read statuses of friends whose houses had been destroyed, or worse, who were missing family members.

Meg couldn't get back to sleep, but she didn't want to wake everyone. She waited until six a.m., and then called her sister.

"Hey," she said in a loud whisper. "I want to go to my house now. I want to collect as much as we can. I want to try and get my computer, if it's not ruined. Can you take me?"

"Yeah," she said, her voice loud in the quiet of the room. "I'll be right there."

The two sisters headed back to Meg's house. They had to park about four blocks away because the roads were closed or congested. The area was unrecognizable. Without street signs, trees, or other familiar landmarks, it all looked the same.

"I have no idea where we are," Meg said, hating to admit she didn't know her own neighborhood.

They jogged around a bit before Meg spotted her house. "There! There we are."

The house looked worse in the daytime than it had the night before. Meg stared at what had been their home, the place they cherished and loved. She lay down on the driveway and cried. When she got up, nausea hit her, and she vomited in the dirt.

"All right," she said, spitting several times. "I'm ready to get to work."

One of the first things she found was her jogging stroller. She and Eileen used it like a wheelbarrow, carting things from the house to the car several blocks away. She found the computer and lots of kids' toys.

Everything was wet. It had rained all night and was still raining. Meg didn't know if anything was usable, but she had to try.

"Looters have been here," Elaine said.

"How do you know?"

Eileen poked a pile of cigarettes with her toe. "Unless you and Scott started smoking. Or maybe the tornado pooped it there?"

Meg felt one corner of her mouth lift in a smile. The whole family had taken to the term her children had given tornado damage. "All right, all right. Did they take anything?"

Eileen shrugged. "How should I know? I don't even know what you took."

The rain began to fall harder and ruined their rescue efforts. It came down in buckets, soaking the two sisters to the bones.

"We need to go, Meg," Eileen said, holding a piece of cardboard over her head. "It's too wet."

Meg ran into the garage, trying to take cover. There was no roof and nothing stopped the rain from coming down. Desperation fueled her, and Meg kicked piles of rubble aside, looking for anything more than could be saved.

"Meg!" Eileen appeared in the garage. Trails of rain coursed down her face. "We need to go now! There's no more we can do!"

"Fine." Meg gave up. She'd have to come back later when it wasn't raining.

They piled a few more items into the stroller, and then pushed it down the street, running as fast as they could. Meg had never imagined in her life that she would feel like a refugee with nowhere to go, but that's exactly how she felt.

The Mitchells

When Nellie woke up, she found James still sleeping on the bed next to her. A quick glance at her phone showed that it was almost six a.m. She tiptoed around him and went upstairs, where she found Jill brewing coffee in a nightgown.

"Hi," Nellie greeted, running a hand through her hair. She couldn't remember falling asleep last night, but she knew it had been shortly after James arrived. "What time did we get back with my mom?"

"Around three a.m," Jill said. The dark circles under her eyes reminded Nellie of James's face when he didn't get enough sleep. Jill opened the fridge and put a carton of milk on the table. Nellie sat down to eat a bowl of cereal.

A moment later James came up from the basement, leaning heavily on the railing as he climbed the stairs. "I have to go."

"Go?" Nellie echoed. She wanted nothing more than for him to sit and hold her all day. "But you worked all night."

"And there's more to do. They need me to go to the airport and get food and water." He grabbed a banana and gave Nellie a quick hug. "I'll call you."

"Wait, I might need the car." Nellie tossed aside her cereal. "What if Mom needs to go somewhere? I'll take you to work."

Nellie drove James to St. Freeman's. As he walked away, Nellie caught sight of the St. John's parking lot. She sat in the car for a moment, staring at all the destroyed areas. Taking a deep breath, she turned the car around and headed back to Jill's.

There was nothing to do now but wait. It rained all day, while Nellie and her mother watched TV. Her phone still wasn't working quite right, but sometimes a text or call came through. Everyone wanted to make sure she was okay. The same questions came up over and over again: "What happened? What did you see?"

Nellie knew the experience was important, but it hurt to relive it each time. *I need to write it down,* she thought. *Then I can share it with everyone at once.*

Her eyes burned with exhaustion. She lay on the couch, her eyes opening and closing wearily. She willed herself to fall asleep, but every time she started to, the wind howled outside and rattled the basement windows. Her heart pounded with anxiety, and she couldn't relax.

What would happen to her mother now? She was homeless and disabled. Where was she going to live? Who would care for her? Nellie had no idea where to take her or what to do with her. Nellie took the dog out for a bit, but it was raining, so they didn't stay out very long.

Nellie's mom couldn't get up or down the stairs because of her injury. Jill didn't come down all day. She stayed upstairs with her little girl. Nellie turned on CNN and she and her mom watched it for most of the day.

When her mother fell asleep around one p.m., Nellie got out her laptop and tried to pull up her blog. Of course, no Internet connection. The urge to write down everything she'd experienced over the past two days overwhelmed her. She opened a word document and started typing. She typed everything she'd seen, everything that had happened.

After she finished typing, Nellie took the car out to put gas in it. She bought some food to snack on at Jill's, like beef jerky, chocolate donuts, bananas, and a few sodas. Jill had food like this, but Nellie felt bad mooching off her.

She didn't look forward to going back to the house. She had nothing to do there except feel helpless. Nellie could feel a headache pounding in her temples from lack of sleep. Maybe she'd be successful this time in going to sleep.

Cara Edens' Home

Cara's cell phone pinged, the particular ping that let her know she had a text. Cara reached across the mattress and picked it up. She hadn't taken her contacts out the night before, and the image blurred in front of her eyes. She blinked several times, but her eyes burned.

The message was from her boss. "Internet down. Don't need to come in, b w family. Don't worry abt ths wk unless want to. Let me know if u need anything."

She glanced at her watch. It was almost seven thirty a.m. Stephen still snored on the bed, and Cara remembered that today was his first day of vacation. She laughed out loud. What a way to start.

She changed her clothes and headed into the kitchen, where she called her dad's cell phone.

"Good morning, Cara-bear." His deep voice sounded tired but chipper.

"Hi," Cara replied, warming a bit at the nickname. "You at the house?"

"Yes. Just cleaning up."

"Okay. We'll be right over." Cara went back into the bedroom. Stephen sat on the bed, his tall frame slouched over. He ran a hand through his hair and yawned.

Cara went back for a bowl of cereal. It would have to be Fruity Pebbles today. No time to cook oatmeal. She noticed several new Facebook messages on her phone. She started scrolling through them while she ate.

"Where are you?"

"Are you okay?"

"Cara, thinking of you, wanted to make sure you're fine."

"Just heard about the tornado. Are you guys safe?"

Cara spent the next half hour responding to more than a dozen such messages. There was a message from Stephen's family in North Carolina. They'd heard about the tornado on the news and wanted to make sure everything was all right.

She tried again to call Emily; still just a busy signal. Cara tried Emily's sister. She was a nurse, so Cara figured she'd be trying to help at one of the hospitals in the area. No answer.

Stephen appeared in the doorway, also in a clean set of clothes. "I'm ready to go when you are."

Cara stowed her phone in her back pocket and stood. "Let's go."

Outside it was raining. Stephen turned the windshield wipers on full blast and Cara gritted her teeth, hating that she couldn't see very well. Another tornado could creep up on them and she wouldn't even see it. She strained her ears, but all she heard was the swish of the wipers. She turned on the radio. The newscaster reported that they wouldn't play any music today, but instead take calls from those searching for loved ones, and keep the public informed about new developments. Cara found the same was true on every station.

She had to show her ID at a police checkpoint to get her and Stephen into the devastated area close to her parents' house. Perhaps because the police weren't letting everyone in, they were able to park closer to her parents' demolished house this time. Her father stood in the yard, directing people as they helped move debris and search for valuables. Glass crunched under Cara's tennis shoes as she stepped up to her dad.

"What would you like us to do?"

Rain dripped down on them, and he wiped water from his eyes. "We're lifting walls, checking to see if there's anything underneath. Can you do that?"

"Sure."

Cara couldn't believe the number of people there to help. Some she recognized as friends and neighbors, but many she'd never seen before. She found her mom, gave her a quick hug. "Where'd all these people come from?"

Her mom shrugged. "They just showed up. People keep driving down the road, asking if we need help. Your dad's boss has been here for almost two hours, helping."

Cara watched her father and various other men load things onto a flatbed trailer. "And where did the trailer come from?"

"One of your dad's coworkers brought it with him."

"Wow." Cara nodded. "Very nice. Where are you putting things? In your storage unit?"

"Yes. No other place for them right now. If we can find the key."

Cara turned, her eyes widening. "You lost the key?"

Her mom sighed. "It was on the corkboard in the kitchen, Cara, where all the keys are hung. If we can find that wall, maybe we can find the key."

Cara shook her head. "No way. I can't believe you think you're going to find it." Still, it was a bit of a challenge, and she made up her mind to search the remains of the kitchen. "Any sign of Indie?" she asked, referring to their pet dog.

"Still nothing. Maybe Stephen can help."

Cara rejoined Stephen as he and Uncle Todd lifted a broken piece of drywall. "My mom wants you to call for the dog. Maybe she'll come to you."

Stephen held the wall steady while Uncle Todd sifted through the contents underneath. "All right. Give me a moment."

"You can go." Uncle Todd stood, brushing his gloved hands on his pants. "I'm done here."

Cara followed Stephen as he walked around the house, whistling and calling for Indie. Then he stopped and held up a hand. "Do you hear something?"

Cara strained her ears. "No. What is it?"

"Sounds like whining." He cupped his hands around his mouth. "Indie! There it is again." He moved forward, visibly excited.

Cara hid her smile. Normally he was not a dog person, but Indie had latched onto him at the right moment.

"Help me here," he grunted, trying to lift a wooden board off of a broken wall.

Now Cara heard the whining too. She joined him, helping him thrust the wood and wall to the ground. Underneath were the washer and dryer, and sitting on top of the dryer, whimpering quietly, was Indie.

"Oh my gosh!" Cara exclaimed. "I can't believe she's okay!"

Stephen gathered her into his arms, where she wagged her tail spastically and licked his face. "She missed me," he chuckled.

They worked all morning, lifting objects and cleaning debris off the lot. Cara never had the chance to feel hungry or thirsty because every ten minutes, someone came by offering water bottles or sandwiches. Besides food items,

185

people offered equipment such as wheelbarrows, shovels, chainsaws. They offered sunblock. A group of people came by giving out over three hundred boxes of diapers, along with baby bottles. Cara's mom quickly snagged some for Caleb.

The family stayed together until it started to get dark. Cara and Stephen said goodnight and then left for their own apartment. The rain had turned nasty, and a strong gale whipped it around their car. As soon as they got into the house, Cara turned on the radio. She bounced her leg up and down, jittery.

"Anything?" Stephen asked from the kitchen. Cara heard the fridge door close.

"More thunderstorms and bad weather," Cara said. She turned the volume up and joined him. Though they had electricity, the cable was still out. Cara hated not being able to check out the radar on The Weather Channel.

An alarm beeped on the radio station seconds before the tornado sirens went off. Stephen swore.

"No," Cara said. She began to shake and pressed her hands over her face. "Not again."

Stephen gripped her shoulders. "Cara, it's okay. We'll be safe."

Cara sobbed into her fingers.

"Come on." Stephen led her into the bedroom.

She shook her head. "No. We need to get into a closet." Their apartment was on the third floor, and Cara knew it simply wouldn't protect them. But she wasn't going to sit on her bed and pretend nothing was happening.

Stephen turned the volume of the radio all the way up. He pulled Cara into the hall closet. He left her alone for a moment, then came back with blankets and a flashlight. He snuggled in next to her, holding her close.

The sirens still sounded, but Cara could hear the newscaster's voice over the sirens. "Get to a safe place. Make sure you have your I.D. Grab a permanent marker and write your contact information on your arm, your leg, anywhere it can be found."

Cara patted Stephen. "Get a marker."

He didn't budge. "We'll be okay."

She didn't have the strength to argue with him. She listened to the DJ's voice telling them to write down their address, birthday, social security number, who you were with, where you were at. "Why do they want us to do that?"

Stephen paused. "The storm didn't always leave people in the same place. Sometimes they were far from home. Sometimes…they weren't in one piece."

Cara closed her eyes, a wave of nausea washing over her at the mental imagery. "Who told you that?"

"Ben."

Stephen's friend Ben worked as a deputy sheriff. Cara hadn't realized they'd talked. She couldn't reach anyone with US Cellular service, and half the time she got busy signals for everyone else, also.

Stephen wasn't finished. "He said they had three hundred body bags, and that wasn't enough. They kept finding more people, and parts of people."

The radio kept talking. "If you've got Facebook on your phone, update your status frequently. Do it now. Tell everyone where you are. Tell them who you're with. Say 'I'm in a closet at home with my sister, my dog,' or whatever."

Did she have her I.D. on her? Cara fished around for her phone. She pulled it from her purse and scrolled through her Facebook page. Her friends' statuses reflected being in closets, or basements, or some other safe place. She pressed her lips together grimly. She doubted anyone stood outside on the balcony watching for the storm tonight. Nobody would be around windows, trying to catch a glimpse.

After more than an hour in the closet, the radio announced that it was safe to come out. Cara hardly believed it. She walked slowly to the bedroom, ready at any moment to bolt back to the closet. Thunder crashed outside and she shuddered.

"I'm going to sleep on the couch."

"Really?" Stephen looked at her. "The bed's just as safe."

Cara twirled her wrist. She'd always done that, even as a child. "Just for tonight."

"I guess it's better than sleeping on the floor. Whatever you want."

Cara nodded, then made her way to the living room. She pulled a blanket up to her chin and listened to the storm. All night it raged. Several times she thought she heard the sirens again, only to realize it was the wind.

Cara covered her ears with her hands and wished for sleep. She'd always hated thunderstorms. Only now it was worse.

Chapter Thirteen

The rest of the week
Approximately 7 days after tornado strike

"We are still here, we have hope, and we will rebuild." –
Morgan Meyer

The Divine Household

When Piper went back to work on Wednesday, she knew she'd never be the same again. The facility hadn't been harmed, but they'd lost an employee. The woman had hidden with her mother and aunt in a closet. Both her mother and aunt survived, but not the woman.

Over thirty families from work had been seriously affected in one way or another. The general manager and the corporate manager put together a fund for any employee who had lost a home. They matched dollar for dollar every donation. Piper gave away everything from home that she didn't need any more, including an old laptop and a lawn mower. She tried to help as many as she could in the first week, though she felt like she was in something of a daze. Life as she knew it had blown to the other side of town. She and her mom went to a number of funerals, which was emotionally trying. They were one right after another.

Piper put in extra hours to help make up for those who weren't at work that first week. Things began to feel more normal. School was out early, but the Boys and Girls Club also opened ahead of schedule, so that made things easier for Piper as far as work and school went.

One of the biggest reliefs for her was finding out that Ashley and her husband were okay. The fire station was

189

destroyed while he was on shift, but he made it out safely. Though Ashley rarely saw him in the days that followed, at least their new family remained intact.

Piper couldn't bring herself to drive through the parts of town that had been obliterated. She was too familiar with Joplin. She couldn't bring herself to go down Twentieth Street. She didn't want to see it.

She still wasn't sleeping right. Adrenaline raced through her blood whenever she lay down, and horrible images played in her mind. Exhaustion muddled her days.

The Borup Family

Nineteen people and four dogs stayed at Melinda's house during the next week. On Tuesday, another Tornado Warning set Joplin on edge. All nineteen people and the dogs sat in the tornado shelter David had built into their house.

The Scaggs Household

Meg spent the rest of the week leaving the kids with her parents and going back to the house with Scott. They took a flatbed trailer with them, and for about three days searched through debris for anything of value. Strangers and volunteers stopped by, helping them search for anything.

Mostly Meg found clothes. She figured clothing could be washed, and her family definitely needed more. *I've got to save this,* she thought. *It's one less thing to buy.* Those thoughts went through her head every time she saw something of potential value.

People drove by in golf carts and threw sandwiches at them. Day by day Meg and Scott worked, and every day volunteers came by with food and drinks. The temperature climbed up into the nineties, and Meg welcomed the Powerades and waters.

"Look at how people react to this," Scott said. "We're in

the thick of it. Look how quickly we set up tents and got organized. It's just...amazing."

"Yeah," Meg agreed.

Stories continued to pour in about friends and family who tried to help the Scaggs after the tornado. Several friends, when they heard that Meg's neighborhood was the hardest hit, ran out on foot to check on them.

"I ran for five blocks, Meg," her 65-year-old boss told her. "And then when I got close to your house, the police stopped me. The block was on fire, and they wouldn't let anyone through."

"I'm so sorry you went through all that!" Meg said, feeling guilty for all the concern people had for her and her family.

"I'm just glad you didn't need me," her boss returned.

Meg continued to hear more stories everyday from her father, who served on the Joplin City Council. The whole week following the tornado was filled with funerals and viewings. In between funerals, Meg worked with Scott and her family to finish salvaging their house.

The week went by in a blur. It felt crazy and insane to Meg. She couldn't wait for this time in her life to be over.

The days after the tornado were especially hard for her to be a parent. The children didn't understand what had happened.

"Where are my toys?" Lizzie would ask. "Where's my bed?"

When Meg would try to explain, Lizzie would grasp the fact that her things were gone, but she couldn't understand why.

Besides her family, Meg had to deal with insurance assessors, and trying to make sure they received the right compensation for their loss. Looters stole everything the Scaggs hadn't saved already: the motorcycle, all of Scott's military gear, credit cards. They left their beer cans all over the garage. It took a few days for the insurance adjuster to get there. The insurance company couldn't have been easier to work with. The adjuster wrote them a check for the damage and stolen goods right then. After seeing the ugly side of humanity, the gesture reminded Meg of the good in people.

Friends stopped by her parents' house frequently with goody bags and kind words. Meg felt grateful every time someone did.

Toward the end of the week, Meg received a strange phone call. She recognized the Kansas City area code, but not the caller. She hesitated a moment before answering. Meg felt burned out from all the police phone calls and reports she'd given. She'd given her information out pretty freely to the press, and it seemed like everyone was calling.

But for some reason, Meg answered. It turned out to be a well-known artist from Kansas City. "I'm making several art projects out of the debris from Joplin," he told her, "to help portray how something beautiful can come out of something tragic. Can we go through the remains of your house?"

Meg just wanted this to end. But she decided to give it a shot. "Sure, why not. Do what you need to do."

The Mitchells

Though no one was required to go into work, on Tuesday Nellie requested to come in. Really, she wanted to use the Internet. Her house still had no electricity, and she couldn't really stay at Jill's all day watching TV with her mom. She didn't even have a good phone signal.

Out of frustration, she called her boss.

"Of course you can come in," her boss said. "But you don't have to."

"I want to," Nellie said. She would go stir-crazy if she stayed here any longer.

But she didn't want to burden Jill with babysitting her mother. Nellie called a coworker whose husband stayed at home during the day.

"Sure he'll watch your mom," her friend said. "You need to be able to go back to work."

Nellie dropped her mom off and then drove to what was left of the apartment. Rain still fell freely on the furnishings. Nellie went through drawers, searching for important papers. She found baby books, bills, photos, and phone numbers.

As soon as she got to the school, Nellie went to work. Besides the job-related activities, she had a million phone calls to make. She called the numbers on her mom's bills and shut off the utilities. All of the pictures and baby books were water damaged, so she laid them out on tables to dry. Already mold spread its black fingers across the pages. She uploaded her blog post, giving everyone an insider's view to the tornado. She needed to figure out how to help her mom. She called a friend in Kansas and asked her to meet her at the school.

"Listen," Nellie said, "I need bras, underwear, and sweatpants. For my mom. Walmart is gone and the other stores are completely packed. I don't have time to get her some, and she doesn't have any."

"Sure," her friend said.

Her friend met her at the school with the clothing for her mom. "Joplin is a mess," she said, her eyes wide. "What happened? What was it like?"

Weariness slapped Nellie across the face, and she struggled to keep her face passive. "Go read my blog. I can't talk about this anymore."

Her friend looked sympathetic and nodded. "Of course. I understand.

The hospital had given Nellie's mom a prescription, but Nellie couldn't find a pharmacy in Joplin that wasn't closed or blown down. Finally, she found one in Webb City that had what she needed. Nellie taught two classes, then drove to Webb City to get the medicine.

Toward the end of the day, Nellie got a very welcome phone call from James.

"I'm at our house," he said, "and the electricity's back on."

"Yes!" Nellie cried. She picked her mom up and hurried home, anxious to put her life in order again. Logging onto Facebook, she posted a quick message: "We're okay but in desperate need of a bed, sheets, and dog food. If you have extra, please send."

Taking her mom to the spare bedroom, she laid out a sleeping bag and several blankets. "This is all I've got for now, Mom."

"I know, honey." Her mom patted her elbow. "It's fine for me."

Nellie started cleaning out the fridge, since most of the food had gone bad. Then her phone started dinging with Facebook messages. She scrolled through them, a state of shock descending upon her. Everyone was responding. All of her friends wanted to help.

Sirens blared outside, and Nellie dropped her phone with a gasp. "James?" she called.

He bolted into the kitchen. "Tornado sirens."

Nellie's stomach pitched. "No. Not again."

"Come on." James opened the hall closet and pulled out a duffel bag. He ran around the house, throwing random bits of food and important documents inside. "Let's go downstairs."

Nellie's hands shook as she stepped down the narrow staircase to the basement. "What about my mom? How will I get her down here?" Her mom still had a borrowed wheelchair and a pair of crutches, but that wouldn't help her down the stairs.

"I'll get her."

Another tornado. Nellie wanted to throw up. How could they withstand this?

James descended the stairs, carrying her mom. The three of them huddled in the basement for more than half an hour before the Tornado Warning was lifted. Nothing hit the city.

The next few days were the worst for Nellie. By Wednesday, classes were back in full session. James still had to go to work, only now he worked extra hours. Nellie packed them lunches and tried to ease his burden, but she knew he was stressed. She bought her mom a prepaid phone so they could keep in touch during the day.

Friends and family still called, always asking how they could help. Most of the time, Nellie didn't know what to tell them, but when her cousin Ben called from Texas, she had an idea.

"Here's how you can help me, Ben," she said. "I need you to call around. Find out what places will take a disabled woman who gets financial assistance. Look at HUD housing. But she's got a dog, too, Ben, so make sure they take a dog."

Ben laughed. "At least you don't ask too much. Anything else?"

"Yes," Nellie said, on a roll. "It needs to be within fifty miles of Joplin."

"You got it."

Ben called back just a few hours later. "I found a place in Carthage. But it's going to go fast. Get your act together and turn in an application by Friday."

Nellie got an application for her mom turned in on time, but she worried the place wouldn't work out. She spent the weekend looking at houses and talking to landlords. Nothing seemed promising, and she began to worry that her mom would be with them for several more weeks.

Cara Edens' Home

The next few days flew by in a blur. The amount of aid and support was overwhelming. Cara could hardly fathom the number of strangers who had come from Texas, Arkansas, even Colorado, overnight to help the tornado-stricken city. They always had at least four other volunteers, and at one point Cara counted fourteen. It made her feel like it didn't matter how far away people were, some would always be willing to help. Cara felt some of the weight lift off her shoulders. The tragedy almost seemed to bind them together.

She still hadn't heard from her friend, Emily.

Each day Cara spent some time searching in the kitchen. She moved boards and broken dishes and debris. She couldn't possibly imagine how she'd find the key to the storage shed in all this.

"Look at this," Mrs. Eden said, and she started to cry. Cara couldn't tell what the muddy object in her hand was. She ran over to her mom.

"Your baby books," her mom said, and she showed Cara the sodden, water-damaged books. She hugged them to her chest and sobbed.

Cara blinked back tears. "At least you found them, Mom. We'll get them cleaned up."

They continued sorting things. Cara went back to searching for the key. Her hands closed on something long and metallic, and she pulled up a butter knife. She tossed it and kept searching. She pulled up a floorboard and stared. A small key with a plastic ring that said "storage" sat wedged between the molding and the floor. "Mom!" she hollered. "You're not going to believe this!"

Everyone cheered when Cara produced the key. It was the only one they ever found.

After that, Cara started in the bedrooms. She found a box of baby clothing close to where her mom had found the baby books.

"Those are the dresses I brought you and your sister home from the hospital in," her mom said when Cara pointed them out.

"We can wash these," Cara said, putting them back. "These things can be saved."

"Oh!" Julie cried. "Andy and Annie!"

"I'd forgotten about those!" Cara exclaimed, examining the rag dolls Grandma Bernice had made for her and Julie.

196

A little after noon, the sky started to darken with gray clouds. It had been gloomy all day, with rain falling off and on. But around three p.m., it began looking quite scary. Cara and her family loaded up what they could in trucks and the trailer. They drove over to the storage unit her parents had rented. Thunder rumbled overhead, and Cara moved quickly from the unit to the trailer, hauling things inside.

Thunder rumbled again and the clouds broke open, dropping an angry rainstorm on them.

"Let's get out of here!" Cara's father shouted.

Everyone piled back into the vehicles and drove off.

Though rain and storms continued to plague recovery efforts, no more tornadoes came through, much to Cara's relief. Dreams of summer vacation in St. Louis drifted away to helping her parents organize their ruined things.

The radio stations were a lifeline. Telephones and Internet were still down, for the most part, and it was one of the only ways to know how things were progressing.

On Thursday, Emily called. Cara stopped and stared at her phone in absolute shock, hardly able to believe it had rung. Shaking off the surprise, she answered it.

"Emily?" Cara exclaimed, thrilled to hear from her friend. She'd worried so much about her and the baby. "How are you? Are you okay?"

"Sorry to keep you worrying," Emily said. "I'm at my mom's house. I've been a bit…distracted."

Her voice sounded off, kind of hollow. Cara felt a prickle of worry. "Is everyone all right, Emily?"

"We're fine. The baby's fine. Adam's working around the clock. I hardly see him."

Adam was a police officer. Cara imagined he was needed a lot right now. Still, Emily sounded so sad. "And your mom and dad? They're okay?"

"Yes." Emily gave a strangled sound, then burst into sobs. "Cara, it's so awful. The bank was destroyed." Emily worked at Commerce Bank. "It's gone. People died, Cara.

People I know. We were at home, and we stayed in the bathtub with a mattress over our heads, and we made it. But others didn't."

Cara cried with her, the hot tears trailing down her face. They wept for those who hadn't survived, and for those who had, who had to live each day knowing someone they loved was gone. It felt good to cry for someone else.

On Friday Cara went into work for the first time. She got caught up on billing, timesheets, and filing. She wasn't the only employee there, but she might as well have been. It was so quiet. Even her coworkers didn't have much to say. They sat at their desks, doing what work they had. Sneaking glances at them, Cara recognized the numb, shocked expression as the same one that greeted her every morning in the mirror. It didn't feel right to participate in the normal behavior of listening to music, laughing and chatting. Everything had changed.

Oddly enough, Cara found it comforting. They all shared this experience. Cara barely spoke to anyone that day, but she felt a bond between her and the other survivors.

The McMinn Family

Kayla and Justin spent the next week in a hotel in Miami, Oklahoma, courtesy of her father. A storm blew in Monday night, and there was talk of a tornado in Miami.

Kayla called the front desk. "I need another mattress brought up, a small one."

"We don't have any small mattresses. Would you like a roll-a-bed?"

"No, no." Kayla hung up, pulling her fingers. What would she put over the bathtub if a tornado blew through? Kayla had never felt so scared in her life. Knowing what might be coming made it ten times worse. Thankfully, nothing more than a severe thunderstorm developed.

FEMA came out two days after Justin called them. They evaluated the destruction of their house, but it still took a week to bring a trailer and clear away the trash. Plans were made to begin construction for a new house on the same plot of land.

Her mom came and stayed with them for a few nights, helping to control the children in the tiny hotel room. Kayla felt incredibly grateful to her father for helping them out with a place to stay. He came by and checked on them every day and every night to make sure they were all right.

The Jason Residence

Monday night, Penny lay tucked into Pierre's side. The low light of the television cast a blue hue over the recliner where her mother sleep.

"We haven't seen Bella," Penny whispered, her fingers stroking Pierre's arm. "What do you think happened to her?"

Pierre tightened his grip on her. "I don't know. I'm sure she's okay."

Which of course, Penny knew he wasn't. But what else could he say? Penny sighed and changed the subject. "It was real sweet of Mom's neighbor to give us that fifty dollars. We can get something else to wear, maybe shoes that fit."

Pierre chuckled, a deep rumble in his chest that tickled her back. "What, you don't like my shoe?"

Penny laughed too, though tears leaked out as well. They fell silent, and Penny closed her eyes. They were alive, they'd survived, and they'd get through this somehow.

Tuesday morning arrived with no rain. Pierre and Penny drove their rental car back over to the remains of the house.

"Everything's ruined," Penny said, pulling soggy, ripped shirts out of broken drawers. "Is there anything worth saving?"

"I found a photo album." Pierre tried to wipe the dirt from the plastic covering. He opened the album and cast a quick glance at Penny. "The pictures are a little wet. Some

199

color bleeding. But they're here."

Penny took the book from him and pressed the tips of her fingers to the faces of her children when they were small. Yes, the photos were damaged, but it was better than nothing. She hugged the album to her chest and carried it back to the car.

Pierre picked up pieces of a bookshelf and Penny threw ruined couch cushions to the side. A noise in the mountain of debris beneath her feet caught her attention. "Did you hear that?"

"Hear what?" Pierre grunted.

"Like a whine. High-pitched." She bent her head near the rubble, straining to hear again. There it was! "No, like a bark!" Penny began shoving things aside without even checking them over. "Bella! Bella, is that you?"

"Penny," Pierre said in a warning tone. "It can't be."

Penny ignored him. The bark came again, and she dug faster.

And there Bella was, pushing her way out of a hole that dropped into the basement. Matted fur clung to her body, but the large bushy tail wagged her entire rear end happily as she pushed her dry nose into Penny's hands and face.

"Bella!" Penny cried again, hugging Bella around her neck. "I can't believe you survived! You little trooper!"

Pierre joined her, scratching Bella behind her ears and her neck. Bella moved away from him, sniffing through the debris until she found a broken canister filled with doggie biscuits.

"Let's get her back to your mom's house," Pierre said. "She's hungry. And we need to make sure she's okay."

"Agreed." This was enough salvaging for today, anyway. Wiping her tears, she guided Bella to the rental car.

The routine was the same for the next week: they'd go to the house and dig through rubble. Every day different groups of people came by to help. Cousins, friends, and neighbors came to dig. Volunteers appeared with backhoes. Church members arrived with drinks and sandwiches.

Pierre found lots of shoes and shirts.

"Can we save these, Penny?" he asked, showing her the dirty clothes.

Penny hesitated. She knew how much Pierre's classy wardrobe meant to him. "Yes. But we need to get them washed."

"They have a laundry facility set up in the Walmart parking lot," one of the volunteers said. "You bring your clothes to them, they wash them, and you get them the next day. It's called 'Tide Loads of Hope' or something like that."

"Oh, that's great," Penny said, throwing the clothes into a box. "We'll do that."

"Look what I found here!" a young man called out, six days after the tornado, pulling a slender, mud-covered cabinet out of the dirt. "Any of these important?" He opened the mirrored-facade, revealing small orange bottles with white lids.

"Well, look at that." Pierre grinned and hobbled over. "All my meds."

Penny joined him, shaking her head in disbelief. "How on earth? That's almost two hundred dollars worth." And way more valuable than the dollar amount.

Pierre pulled the bottles from the cabinet. "Maybe we'll find your ring after all."

Chapter Fourteen

June 2011
Approximately one month after tornado strike

"I thank the stars above that I still have my family and now I try to cherish every moment I can." — Michelle Short

The Divine Household

Several weeks went by before Piper broke down and went to the doctor. She couldn't sleep. Every time she lay down, she pictured those women who didn't make it. In her mind, the women became her friends. Even though Piper hadn't been in the tornado, nightmares plagued her. She saw people crawling out of debris moments after the tornado hit.

She relived over and over again the chaotic moments where nobody knew what was happening. Nobody knew how bad the damage was. These were things she'd never forget.

The drive to the doctor was also the first time that Piper actually drove through Joplin since the tornado. She gave herself a pep talk on the way out of the house, telling herself this was something she needed to do. Still, she had a hard time focusing her breathing.

To her relief, downtown was totally different than the night of the disaster. There weren't people with gashes wandering around, people crawling out of rubble. While still destroyed, everything was calmer. Piper relaxed a bit, content with the feeling that life moved on, things were getting better. It was still hard to look at. This was her town. Piper had grown up in Joplin. The landmarks that had always been there, such as the hospital, the elementary school, were gone. From Range Line, she could see the hospital shell. Nothing obstructed the view. The sight was disconcerting.

The doctor diagnosed her with PTSD, or post-traumatic stress disorder. He gave her a prescription. It took almost a month after seeing the doctor before Piper noticed that the nightmares were lessening and she could deal better with the guilt. Storms were easing up as well, as summer came on and the rainy season dried up.

Michael could not understand why school was out for the summer. He had been so absorbed in his book that he hadn't really noticed what was going on. His school wasn't damaged. He simply couldn't understand why he couldn't go back and see his friends again.

At the Boys and Girls Club, Michael began to comprehend the tragedy. There were kids there who had been in the middle of the whole thing. Several times Michael came home with questions. Why was his house fine when others lost everything?

Piper was glad he had been shielded from the disaster. She didn't want him to have those images in his mind.

Michael left for his dad's house at the beginning of June, to stay for the summer. With him gone, Piper found herself with extra time on her hands. She began volunteering at the Red Cross and other organizations. She carried a lot of guilt for not being able to help anyone on the night of the tornado. Volunteering at the Red Cross helped her feel better. Piper felt a tremendous drive to give back and help those who weren't as lucky as her.

By the middle of July, Piper felt like things were mostly back to normal.

The Borup Family

Melinda and her family were lucky in that their house wasn't destroyed. But they spent the next several weeks involved with relief efforts and giving aid to those who hadn't been so lucky.

Many members of Melinda's church lived outside of Joplin. For months the youth of Joplin and surrounding cities had been planning a group trip to Illinois. After the tornado, it became clear that several of the Joplin teenagers wouldn't have the funding to make such a trip. In an act of good will, the church leaders made arrangements to help as many youth as possible make the trip.

Their efforts panned out. More than 200 Joplin teens joined the church group for the trip to Illinois. Everywhere they went, as soon as people realized where they had come from, the youth were met with compassion and caring. Melinda's husband said the experience was very sacred, and he would never forget the kindness of strangers reaching out to them.

The Scaggs Household

Meg and her family moved out of her parents' house and moved in with her sister. It was wonderful to have a place to stay, but they were still intruding on someone else's space. Eileen went back to work, leaving Meg alone with the children during the day.

The children were clingy and whiny. They followed Meg around the house, holding onto her sleeves, her hands, her clothes. Meg had to stay by their sides for a good three weeks before they started to calm down. She didn't really expect them to be stable; she was an emotional wreck, and she knew they fed off her emotions. Some days she sat on the couch and cried. Others, she could barely get herself out of bed.

At Eileen's house, they finally began to settle into a routine. The initial shock wore off, and everyone began to calm down. Meg could see that the children needed security and love if they were going to adjust, so she worked hard to give it to them. She signed them up for the kids' art classes at Spiva. Lizzie took several classes, and the projects were good for her, helping her to focus on something besides the tragedy. Even Nick did a few, just to go and do art helped him calm down. The children craved normalcy, and the art classes provided that.

Meg and the artist from Kansas City met out at the remains of her house to start the project. He remained very professional and respectful through it all. He picked out kids' toys and broken pieces of the dining room table. The table especially meant something to Meg, as she and her husband had just bought the ten-person table one week before the tornado. It was a huge loss to them.

The artist also picked up a globe paperweight he found in Meg's garage.

"Oh," Meg said, remembering the globe. "My boss in California gave that to me. It sat on my desk for two years while I worked for his photography studio." The thought that the globe might still serve an aesthetic purpose warmed Meg inside.

After going through the debris at her house, they went over to her boss's house. Along the way, the artist stopped and examined things in the street. Meg almost laughed when they found one of her strawberry plants, several houses away from her garden. The pot was a Christmas gift from her parents, several years ago. The artist took it as well. Meg thought the experience was an uplifting one, almost cathartic. As an artist herself, it inspired her to finally see the beauty in the things they had lost. Things that she had thought of as trash were now art. It wasn't rubble she owned, but something valuable.

The trek through the house took an hour. The whole process was a healing one for Meg.

The artist took her things to the Lady Vocus Gallery in Kansas City, where several other artists chose pieces of the debris to make artwork. The art was then auctioned off to help raise money for Spiva and artists who had lost their homes. The project received tons of press attention.

The auction turned out to be a huge event. Meg and her family were invited, first because Meg worked for Spiva, and second because of her help in getting the art pieces for the auction. There were seven artists present who had lost their homes. The art pieces were auctioned off during a live event in Kansas City called "Twist and Shout."

Sherry Peak Roberts made a beautiful angel with the globe, using the globe as the skirt. The body was formed from pieces of broken furniture. Meg immediately fell in love with the art piece. She introduced herself to the artist.

"That was my globe," she said. "I love what you've done with it. It's beautiful."

"Oh!" Sherry said. "How wonderful to meet you! I'm so glad you like it."

Sherry and Meg bonded over the art piece. When Meg joined Scott and her family, she said, "I'd like to buy the globe angel."

They saw several art pieces they liked, including a lovely one that had been made with Meg's strawberry planter. But they stayed quiet, waiting for the angel globe. When it finally came, Meg was shocked at the prices it fetched. As the auction price went up past a thousand dollars, she knew that she couldn't buy it. While it disappointed her, Meg felt a sense of pride that something she owned could be so valuable and beautiful.

The auction raised over $26,000 to help Spiva artists who had lost their homes.

A few weeks after the auction, Sherry Roberts contacted Meg.

"You liked the angel so much; I know you wanted it for yourself, so I'm making you another one with the other side of the globe."

Meg pressed a hand to her mouth and laughed, feeling tears sting her eyes. "Oh, Sherry! That's wonderful! Thank you so much!"

TAMARA HART HEINER

The Mitchells

The housing in Carthage panned out, and Nellie's mom moved out two weeks after the tornado. Many of her friends still had displaced family members living with them, and Nellie felt incredibly grateful to Ben for helping her find a place for her mom.

On Memorial Day weekend, Nellie's family drove in to see them. They spent Saturday at her mother's old apartment, saving everything they could. Everything had been rained on for a week, and it was a mess. Some of the laundry could be saved, but not much else.

Saturday night several friends came over as well. They met at another family member's house, and the cousins saw each other for the first time since the tornado. They drove out to the practice field at the high school, a place that had been destroyed by the tornado. They stood out there with the damage all around them and took family pictures. The pictures represented people who were still thriving in spite of the horrible devastation around them.

Cara Edens' Home

Cara struggled to come to grips with the tragedy around them over the next few weeks. The only way she managed to drive through the devastated area was by building up an emotionless wall around her. She couldn't think or feel or even look at the destruction, or she'd break down.

She reminded herself every day that she still had her family. But even that often made her think of how close she had come to losing them. If she and Stephen had gone to dinner with her parents, or if her sister hadn't been working, there wouldn't have been room in the closet. The thought would leave her shaking and breathless.

Eventually, she and Stephen came to the realization that they needed to move. Cara couldn't get past this. She realized that "a lot of the things you own are just exactly that, things. You can replace them, even if it's your favorite TV or couch or shirt, they can all be replaced." Coming face-to-face with the losses on a daily basis made it hard for Cara to live in the present. Though grateful for the perspective on life the tornado gave her, she wanted to be able to move on with it.

The Jason Residence

It took two weeks for the car insurance to approve the Jasons' insurance claims on the cars, which were finally declared total losses. Several community groups volunteered time and money to help out people like Penny and Pierre. Between these different groups, their church, and Penny's job, they were able to receive the money they needed for new cars and rent. Their house, which was also a rental, had no insurance on it, so everything within was lost as well.

The youth group director from their church took Penny's stepdaughter out on a shopping spree to buy new clothes and school supplies before her sophomore year of high school started. People continue to pour out generosity and support to Pierre and Penny long after the tornado ended.

Even though it was crowded at Penny's mother's, at least they had a place to stay. For six weeks they lived in a one-room apartment. Her stepdaughter went back and forth between her mother and father, not really settling in any one place. Penny and Pierre collected the belongings they'd saved and the items they'd received and lived out of boxes.

They never did find Penny's ring.

Chapter Fifteen

April 2012
Approximately one year after tornado strike

"Even though everyone had lost every last bit of what they loved, they still gave everything they could to help each other."
— Angel Inthurm

The Mitchells

Nellie's mom never wanted to leave Joplin. Today she's a twenty-five minute drive away in Carthage. Though Nellie knows how lucky her mom was to find housing, she misses not having her a mile and a half away. She used to drive by her house every day. The little dog, who survived a tornado, succumbed to a back injury just two weeks after the move. Now her mother lives in a strange city without her family, and no dog.

In spite of the bad things, Nellie's life is good. She tries not to dwell on the hard stuff and just keeps going. Her house is okay and she likes to think everything's okay now.

Nellie and her husband still bike around town. The middle is something of a ghost town; no traffic lights, no houses. It's like the tornado wanted to leave behind a message. After the tornado it smelled old, broken, rotten. Now the city smells of new construction, new wood. It's almost like a rebirth.

The McMinn Family

Kayla and Justin live in Joplin, on the same plot of land but in a new house that FEMA built for them. FEMA took care of them, giving them $8,000 for expenditures. With this money, they were able to buy a new car, and Justin didn't miss any work.

Even today Kayla is afraid of storms. If it's sunny and the wind blows, it freaks her out. If it's at night, she's afraid to sleep because she might not hear the alarms. It scares her three-year-old as well.

Kayla has a love/hate relationship with the local news channel, which probably knows her voice by heart. Any time it storms, she calls to see if there's a tornado in the area.

"If it happens, we'll post a warning on TV," a newscaster reassured her.

But Kayla doesn't trust the warning system. One time she pestered the news people so much that they hung up on her.

"I don't want just a Tornado Warning," she said. "I want to know the tornado is coming."

"We'll give you plenty of notice," a male newscaster said.

"Like last time?" Kayla demanded. "Plenty of notice before it kills us?"

That was when she got hung up on.

She spends a lot of time listening when it storms. Except the tornado never sounded like a train, not to her. It sounded like thunder that doesn't stop roaring.

But Kayla realized what they meant the next time she got stopped by a train. The rush of wind, the noise a train makes as it hurries by with no horn, that sound is like a tornado. Just the thought makes Kayla shudder.

Justin's mom passed away from cancer in March 2012, just a month shy of the one-year anniversary of the Joplin tornado.

The Divine Household

Today Piper shares an apartment with her mother and

son, Michael. She moved into her mom's apartment when the air conditioning went out in her house. It was meant to be temporary, but Piper and her mom felt it was easier on both of them. It saved money and time, since her mom's apartment is closer to their work. Piper enjoys being with her mom, and Michael especially likes being around Nana.

Life is mostly back to normal for her and her family. She's in school, going to work, and busy being a mom. She feels like she's managing all three roles well. When she drives through the downtown area, Piper winces a little bit. The first time she drove down Range Line at night really got to her because it was pitch black. Piper was used to it being lit up like a lighting bug. She still has dreams from time to time, but not nearly as frequently. When it does storm, Piper has a hard time sleeping because of the thunder and lightning stirring up memories from the back of her mind. The tornado will always be there. It will always impact them.

Because Michael never went through the storm, he isn't having to recover from it the way Piper is. He was only impacted by what others told him, and though that affected him, he never fully grasped everything that happened. Everything important to him still existed.

Piper tries to live more in the moment today than she used to. The tornado impacted her life enough that a few months ago she got a new tattoo. This one shows a little tornado and says, "Heal Heartland, May 22, 2011." The tornado has affected who she is and how she lives. A Joplin native for more than thirty years, Piper still struggles to grasp the reality that half of it is gone.

The most important difference for Piper now is that she constantly tells those she loves that she loves them. She never knows what could happen at any minute.

The Borup Family

Since Melinda's church building was destroyed, she and

the congregation meet in another church's chapel every Sunday. The high school band also lost their practice hall, so they meet in the Memorial Hall. Melinda continues to work closely with the high school students, helping many who were deeply traumatized by the events of the tornado.

David's job went from being regular hours to being on-call. As a radiologist, he's not in high demand in Joplin at the moment. He's home a lot more, which stresses him out. The hours he pulls are often out of town or odd hours, like from ten p.m. to two-thirty a.m. He works odd jobs to make up the dollar difference. Every day is different.

But while their family life is incredibly disrupted, Melinda often feels she has no room to complain. They didn't lose their house, her husband is a doctor, and he still has a job. Still, it's hard to explain the adjustment the family has had to go through. It's not what they're used to.

It could've been worse. Melinda feels very grateful that graduation pulled so many people to the other side of town that night. If everyone had been home, she's certain the death toll would've been higher. Instead of being at the high school practicing or in the shopping district, people were at graduation.

Melinda finds that sleep still alludes her. She takes medication to make the spinning stop. Otherwise, as soon as she closes her eyes, she sees the tornado swirling around her.

The Jason Residence

After a futile attempt to get housing through FEMA, Penny realized it was up to her and Pierre to find a place to go. Today Penny and Pierre are settled in another house with a basement across from her mother's apartment. Penny considers it a blessing for them.

"I love my mom to death, but it was too crowded," she said. One day when leaving the apartment, she saw the guy across the street nailing a sign to the tree. Penny went over and took the "For Rent" sign down before anyone could see it.

"That night I called," Penny said, "I was so excited." The man called her back the next day and said he was managing the property. The house owner lived in Massachusetts and just happened to have this house available.

It was a win-win situation for them. Without even doing a background check or asking for a deposit, the owner told the manager to give them the key. In return, Penny and Pierre helped out with some of the work that needed doing around the house. When the sewer backed up into the basement, they went down in their rain boots and tried to drain it. It turned out that all the sewer pipes were busted and it took two months to get new ones and install the new pump.

Unfortunately, the new house didn't allow dogs. After all she'd been through, Bella and the Jasons had to part ways. A lady from the humane society took pity on Bella and adopted her.

Penny and Pierre are both back to work at their normal jobs. They have cars, and even their stepdaughter is driving now, sharing Penny's car with her. All the high schoolers went to Memorial Hall for school after the tornado destroyed the high school, just a few blocks from their rental. Everyone is well, healthy, and caught up on their meds.

While Penny used to love the occasional thunderstorm, any bad storm bothers her now, especially if the electricity goes out. Or worse, when the sirens go off! She stays up until the storm has passed, sitting in a safe place with all her important belongings around her.

The Scaggs Household

At the end of June, Meg and Scott found out that he was being transferred. They had one week to relocate to Northwest Arkansas. Meg lives in Gravette, Arkansas, with her husband and children. She has had opportunities to speak about the tornado at her daughter's school, using pictures she took to present a slide show of the events and damage. Not a day goes by that she doesn't think about the tornado. It completely changed her. She feels a deep appreciation for her husband and children.

Meg had a lot of anxiety about sending Lizzie to school at all. After the tornado, she wants to have her children around her at all times. She wasn't crazy about any of the schools close by that she visited. Meg couldn't bear the thought of sending her on the bus. Luckily, she found a school in Rogers, Arkansas, that only has classes two days a week. The other three days, Lizzie is homeschooled. Still, Meg thought she would throw up on the first day of school; she was more nervous than Lizzie.

Meg absolutely loves having Lizzie home. She loves homeschooling. Having been very career-oriented before the tornado, Meg would never have believed she'd want to homeschool. She didn't think she had the patience to do such a thing. Meg had a nanny for years to help her run her household and care for the children. She had no idea she was capable of doing all that she does on her own.

Meg still runs whenever she can. While Lizzie does karate, Meg heads to the gym next door and runs on the treadmill. Running is a necessity in her life. Sometimes she thinks about the route she'd run in Joplin. The muffler shop and the house were both leveled in the tornado. She has no idea where the owners are now.

Besides Meg's nervousness about letting Lizzie go to school, the children and even the dog suffer from anxiety since the tornado. Ellie is very jittery now. The first Tornado Warning in Gravette kept Meg up all night. Harris, the baby, still shrieks any time he gets into a bathtub and hears the sound of running water. He tries to claw his way out. The same thing happens when Meg runs the vacuum cleaner.

Some things are better. Meg moves slower, takes more time to enjoy what she's doing. Now that she's not working, she feels a sense of calmness that there are no deadlines hanging over her head. She's happiest and feels the most peace when her family is together.

Meg often saw the kindness of strangers after the tornado, also. Some friends set up a donation account for her family, and donations came in from all across the nation, from people Meg had never met. They got gift cards, boxes of toys, and checks in the mail. She made an Excel spreadsheet so she could keep track of the thank you notes she wrote. The last time she looked, she had written 165 "thank you" notes. The response and generosity of strangers is humbling. It affects Meg every day and makes her strive to be a better person, to find ways to pay it forward.

Meg saw the dark side of humanity after the tornado, but the good side far outweighed the bad.

Cara Edens' Home

Today, Cara's parents and sister live in FEMA trailers given to them by the government. They are waiting for more permanent residences. Her parents are still undecided as to whether they want to rebuild. Cara's mom doesn't want to; she feels there are too many bad memories associated with that particular plot of land now.

Julie's landlord is not rebuilding. The landlord took the insurance money for the destroyed lot and left the city. With no chance for a quick permanent house, Julie may be in her trailer for a while longer.

Cara and Stephen recently moved to Neosho, Missouri. Cara is still going to school, and she just started a new job. She now works as a server at a local pizza place.

She misses being close to her family, especially on Sundays. They haven't had a nice family dinner since before the tornado. But the chance to start over in a new town was too valuable to pass up. The fact that her parents' house is gone contributed, Cara feels. Nobody wants to have Sunday dinner in a different place and recognize definitively that the family gathering place is gone. Cara can't help adding that, "It's tough to see your childhood home destroyed, but if my parents or nephew wouldn't have survived, I would be devastated. I am so thankful God protected that little closet they were in. I feel for each and every person who did lose someone because of that day."

Cara sees a counselor and spends nearly every session talking about the tornado. She still hasn't cried, not the deep-down cry—the kind that pulls all the hurts and angers and puts them out on the table to wash. She thinks if she could just mourn, not superficially but deeply, it would make things at least a little better. It was so much easier to numb out the pain and move forward.

She and Stephen are settling into a new kind of normal. The old normal doesn't exist anymore. Anytime she drives through Joplin to see her family, she drives with tunnel vision. She can't let herself be bothered by what she sees, so she doesn't see it.

There is hope for the future, though. The people who have repaired their houses and are rebuilding have the chance for something fresh and new, and safer. Different organizations have extended their hands to help. Cara loves how the community and the people around them came together to help in whatever way they could. That sense of community was missing before the tornado. It's too bad it took a tragedy to bring it about.

"I just wish I could wave a wand over Joplin and turn time back to before the tornado," Cara says.

Afterword

"It's still hard to accept at times that the things and places I've known all my life are forever gone, wiped out in mere moments." — Michelle Short

If you live in a tornado-prone area, you and your family should have a plan of action. William A. Gallus, a professor of Geological and Atmospheric Sciences at Iowa State University, says, "You should just be sure that your entire family knows what they will do when a Tornado Warning is issued (or they hear sirens if they are in a region that has sirens)."

1) The first step is to decide where your safe place is. "Ideally, have some place in mind in your basement, under a large table." If you don't have a basement, "have an interior closet or bathroom in mind." This room should be on the lowest floor of the building. Hide under a large piece of furniture. Bathtubs with mattresses over them work well as safe places. Stay away from windows! If possible, make sure the room you are hiding in has no windows. Use a closet if necessary.[11]

Roger Edwards, forecaster for the National Weather Service, advises that "if you are planning to build a house, especially east of the Rockies, consider an underground tornado shelter or a concrete-lined interior 'safe room.' Consider obtaining a heavy metal safe to store irreplaceable valuables and documents."

You should also have a designated meet-up place outside the home in case one or more members is not at home or

---

11   HTTP://www.ready.gov/tornadoes

cannot get home. [12]

2) Have an emergency contact. While neighbors and friends are fine, they could also be affected by a regional disaster. Make sure you have a contact who lives out of state and won't be affected by any natural disaster. In case of separation, family members should be instructed to call the contact and let him know where they are. This way each person can be accounted for.[13]

3) Keep your safe place stocked with things you might need. Assemble an emergency kit. Ideally, this should have three days' worth of food and water for each person in your family. It should have copies of important documents such as passports, birth certificates, marriage licenses, and social security cards. Have at least one change of clothing for each person, first-aid supplies, and toiletries. You'll definitely want a flashlight and backup batteries, extra car keys, and money. If any family members have special needs, such as a baby, it should have items for them as well. Keep this in the safe place.[14] It's a good idea to "grab bicycle helmets on the way to your shelter," says Gallus. "If you don't have a basement, it is even more important to grab a bicycle helmet and wear it if you have one." In agreement with that sentiment, Edwards says, "Flying debris is the greatest danger in tornadoes; so store protective coverings (e.g., mattresses, sleeping bags, thick blankets, helmets, etc.) in or next to your shelter space, ready to use in a few seconds' notice."

Check on your emergency kit at least once a year. Children grow, and clothes that fit last year may not fit when the disaster hits![15]

4) Practice. One of the big mistakes people make is assuming it will never happen to them. *It happens.* Assume

---

12   HTTP://www.ready.gov/tornadoes
13   ibid
14   ibid
15   ibid

it will happen and prepare for it as if it will. Edwards says to "practice a family tornado drill at least once a year." One of the biggest tornado myths, according to Gallus, is that "tornadoes will avoid a place, such as a river, lake, hill, mountain, Indian burial ground, etc. Tornadoes have crossed some of the highest Rocky Mountains, the Mississippi River, and multiple steep ridges. NOTHING will stop a tornado."

5) Have a battery-operated radio (such as the NOAA Weather Radio) in the safe place, or take one with you. Keep a map in there so you can follow along with the warnings and know where the tornado is going.[16]

6) Any time you plan a group outing or outdoor adventure, make sure the weather forecast is clear. Even then, the weather can change quickly. Have a safe place in mind where you are going.[17]

7) Learn about the emergency plans that have been established in your area by your state and local government. In any emergency, always listen to the instructions given by local emergency management officials. [18]

Edwards adds that you should "have a tornado plan in place at home and at work, based on the kind of structure you occupy. Know where you can take shelter in a matter of seconds, and have a predetermined place to meet after a disaster. When a tornado watch is issued, think about the drill and check to make sure all your safety supplies are handy. Turn on local TV, radio or NOAA Weather Radio and stay alert for warnings. Don't waste precious seconds opening windows; the tornado will blast open the windows for you! If you shop frequently at certain stores, learn where there are bathrooms, storage rooms or other interior shelter areas away from windows, and the shortest ways to get there."

---

16   ibid
17   ibid
18   ibid

TORNADO WARNING

For Your Emergency Kit:

Try to assemble your kit well in advance of an emergency. You may have to evacuate at a moment's notice and take essentials with you. You will probably not have time to search for or shop for the supplies you need.[19]

You may need to survive on your own after an emergency. This means having your own food, water, and other supplies in sufficient quantity to last for at least 72 hours. Local officials and relief workers will be on the scene after a disaster but they cannot reach everyone immediately. You could get help in hours or it might take days.[20]

Additionally, basic services such as electricity, gas, water, sewage treatment and telephones may be cut off for days, or even a week or longer. Your supplies kit should contain items to help you manage during these outages.[21]

Gallus adds that, "A flashlight, a first-aid kit, and maybe a crowbar for getting out if trapped by debris would be the best things" to have in your safe room.

Extreme windstorms in many parts of the country pose a serious threat to buildings and their occupants. Your residence may be built "to code," but that does not mean it can withstand winds from extreme events such as tornadoes and major hurricanes. The purpose of a safe room or a wind shelter is to provide a space where you and your family can seek refuge that provides a high level of protection. You can build a safe room in one of several places in your home:

• Your basement

• Atop a concrete slab-on-grade foundation or garage floor.

• An interior room on the first floor.[22]

Safe rooms built below ground level provide the greatest protection, but a safe room built in a first-floor interior room

19 ibid
20 ibid
21 ibid
22 ibid

also can provide the necessary protection. Belowground safe rooms must be designed to avoid accumulating water during the heavy rains that often accompany severe windstorms.[23]

A Safe Room

You can opt to have a safe room built into your dwelling instead of choosing a safe place. To protect its occupants, a safe room must be built to withstand high winds and flying debris, even if the rest of the residence is severely damaged or destroyed. Consider the following when building a safe room:

The safe room must be adequately anchored to resist overturning and uplifting.

The walls, ceiling and door of the shelter must withstand wind pressure and resist penetration by wind-borne objects and falling debris.

The connections between all parts of the safe room must be strong enough to resist the wind.

The walls of the safe room must be able to separate from the main residence so that damage to the house will not cause damage to the safe room.[24]

Additional information about Safe Rooms available from FEMA:

Taking Shelter from the Storm: Building a Safe Room Inside Your House. FEMA L-233. Brochure providing details about obtaining information on how to build a wind-safe room to withstand tornado, hurricane and other high winds.

Taking Shelter from the Storm: Building a Safe Room Inside Your House. FEMA L-320. Manual with detailed information about how to build a wind-safe room to withstand tornado, hurricane and other high winds.[25]

---

23   ibid
24   ibid
25   ibid

TORNADO WARNING

"Life moved on, but the rest of us stopped where we were." —
Daisy Crawford

When conditions are right for a tornado, first a Severe Thunderstorm Warning or a Tornado Watch will be issued. Anytime there is a thunderstorm, you should be prepared for it to turn into a tornado.[26] Roger Edwards, a forecaster for the National Weather Service and Storm Prediction Center, says, "Any thunderstorm can be deadly by virtue of lightning or flooding rains, but those don't count as severe for meteorological purposes. To be severe, a thunderstorm needs to have hail an inch or larger in diameter, 58-mph (50-knot) winds, and/or a tornado. The National Weather Service issues four kinds of watches and warnings involving severe thunderstorms:

• **Severe Thunderstorm Watch**: Multiple severe thunderstorms may develop in the next three to eight hours. While a tornado can't be ruled out, hail and/or damaging winds are the main threats. Watches aren't intended to cover isolated, brief, unorganized severe weather. Folks should be alert to the sky, have a way to receive warnings for their locations, and remain near indoor shelter in case of a warning.

• **Tornado Watch**: Multiple tornadoes or at least one strong (EF2) tornado are possible in the watch area in the next three to eight hours, in addition to other kinds of severe weather. Remain near sturdy shelter, and be ready to carry out your tornado safety plan at a moment's notice if a tornado is spotted or a warning is issued.

• **Severe Thunderstorm Warning**: Large hail and/or damaging winds are likely at or near your location within minutes. Safest shelter is indoors, away from windows and doors.

• **Tornado Warning**: A tornado has been spotted or indicated by radar. The storm responsible for it is moving in your general direction and may arrive any minute.

26   Roger Edwards

Immediately take shelter according to your safety plan for wherever you are.[27]

"Severe weather watches are issued by the Storm Prediction Center; warnings come from local National Weather Service offices."[28]

Professor Gallus adds, "A Severe Thunderstorm Warning means a severe storm is happening. A watch means that conditions are right so that the event 'might' happen later. Thus a tornado watch means a tornado could happen later."

Be on your guard. Watches don't always turn into warnings, but when they do, it can happen very quickly. "Warnings mean that the event is actually happening," says Gallus. "So a Tornado Warning means a tornado has been spotted, or radar shows swirling winds that could be a tornado. A warning is thus more serious than a watch."

Listen to the National Weather Service radio or some other early notification system. The NOAA Weather Radio is the best way to get early warnings from the National Weather Service. Gallus explains that "A NOAA Weather Radio provides continuous weather information — usually it is roughly a five to seven minute broadcast cycling over and over with the forecast, current conditions, etc." These radios are special because "when a warning is issued (such as a Tornado Warning), an alarm goes off and thus you know instantly that there is a warning. In some of them, after the alarm sounds, the broadcast begins and you hear all the details. In others, you might have to then click on a button yourself to hear details."[29]

Edwards further says that, "Weather radios are specifically tuned to twenty-four hour broadcasts of forecasts and warnings on a designated frequency. You can listen to local forecasts and conditions at any time of day or night. Every modern weather radio can be programmed to

27   ibid
28   ibid
29   William Gallus

pick up warnings of your choosing for your county, as well as others nearby. When operated with a working battery, they can alarm at any hour for warnings, regardless of power outages. If a Tornado Warning happens at three a.m. with the power out, and the radio and battery are working right, you'll get that warning right away with a loud alarm." These radios can be purchased in many stores.

Alerts and actions you should take:

SEVERE THUNDERSTORM WATCH: Severe thunderstorms are possible in your area.

SEVERE THUNDERSTORM WARNING: Severe thunderstorms are occurring. Stay indoors and away from windows.

TORNADO WATCH: Tornadoes are possible in your area. Remain alert for approaching storms.

TORNADO WARNING: A tornado has been sighted or indicated by weather radar. If a Tornado Warning is issued for your area, don't wait for the sky to become threatening. Move to your pre-designated place of safety.[30]

If you are under a severe thunderstorm watch or warning, be observant of the weather. Even if there is no warning, seek shelter at the first sign of a tornado.[31]

Know What to Watch For

"The sound the tornado made is indescribable, it was so intense and loud, like the entire earth was rumbling and roaring in anger." — Michelle Short

Tornadoes usually give warning signs before they occur. You might not know what to look for, as they "have a huge variety of looks," says Professor Gallus. "Some can be narrow, some wide. The narrow ones might look exactly like the Wizard of Oz one. Wide ones can look like a wall of black moving in, and might be mistaken as just a lot of

30   ibid
31   ibid

rain. They can look white if you are facing away from the direction of the sun. Otherwise, they will look dark."

If you see a tornado, "if it is far away, you might try to determine what way it is moving, and if it is not moving toward you, you can stay where you are."[32] But Gallus adds that, "unless you are absolutely sure of that, you should take shelter." It's also important to contact local authorities, such as through 911, to report what you've seen. "You can also call the National Weather Service to report it, but usually local authorities will relay your message to them," Gallus says.

Many people think they will see a tornado approaching. But some tornadoes are hard to see because of rain, clouds, or darkness. Night is one of the deadliest times for a tornado to hit because they are nearly invisible. Even though it hit in the early evening, the Joplin tornado looked like a giant wall of rain. It was so wide that many didn't even see the funnel.[33]

Because of this, there are other warning signs of a tornado to be aware of. "Some signs of it approaching might be large hailstones falling," says Gallus. "Usually the tornado hits shortly after the large hail stops falling," giving you a brief window of opportunity to get to your safe place, from the moment the hail begins to the moment the tornado hits.[34] He adds that, "You might also feel pressure changes in your ears, but that tends to happen right when the tornado is about to hit, so you'd have only a few seconds to do anything. If you see lots of flashes that are bluish or bluish-green, that could be a sign of transformers exploding. People sometimes accidentally think that is just lightning."

In addition, you should watch out for:
- A very dark sky, which may appear green in color
- A loud roar, often compared to that of a train rushing

---

32   ibid
33   ibid
34   ibid

by[35]

"The best warning sign for an approaching tornado," says Edwards, "is a Tornado Warning. That might sound obvious, but it really is important to have a reliable way to receive warnings directly, no matter where you go, on any day when severe storms are possible in the area. Visible signs include the cloud base of a thunderstorm moving rapidly in a circle (rotation). Even if no debris can be seen under the rotation, a tornado could form there at any time. At night, a roaring noise or increasingly loud rumble (not temporary like thunder) could be either a damaging wind or tornado approaching."

If you see or hear any of these signs, the tornado is very close! Make sure you have on a good pair of shoes and seek shelter immediately![36]

When the Tornado Hits

"In the middle of a tornado," Gallus says, "about all you can do (besides pray) is keep your head shielded, and try to lie as low to the ground as you can, and maybe hang onto something." Get under a sturdy table and use your arms to protect your head and neck. Hopefully you and your family already have your emergency kits and your emergency plan. Get to your safe room and sit tight.[37] "Any safe room-type shelter should be best for a tornado," Gallus remarks. If you don't have access to a basement, "The interior room or bathroom or bathtub is a little safer, but not a terribly good shelter." If you're in the bathroom, the best thing to do is "lie in the tub and have a mattress over your body and head, and maybe a bike helmet on." Even in a basement, "it is not a great shelter to just be standing in the open, or near any window." Keep away from all windows, and do not open them.[38]

35   HTTP://www.ready.gov/tornadoes
36   Roger Edwards
37   William Gallus
38   ibid

If your house is a mobile home, however, "there is NO PLACE safe," warns Gallus. Get out immediately and go to the lowest floor of a sturdy, nearby building or a storm shelter. Mobile homes, even if tied down, offer little protection from tornadoes. Edwards says that the same can be said for "portable buildings, RVs, campers, sheds or any temporary structures."

If you are in a building that is not your home, follow their designated safety procedures. In a high-rise building, get to the lowest level. Stay away from corners, windows, doors, and outside walls, if at all possible. Put as many walls as possible between you and the outside. Hallways in commercial buildings are often safer than rooms.[39] Dr. Greg Forbes, the tornado expert from The Weather Channel Companies, says to "avoid large-span roof areas such as school gymnasiums, arenas, or shopping malls."

This assumes you're lucky enough to find yourself indoors. "No place outdoors is safe," Gallus admits. But if you are outside, you can still take precautions. You should:

1) Seek shelter indoors, if at all possible. This could be a basement or a study structure.[40] Dr. Forbes adds that "once you are in a safe location, call or text family members to make sure they seek shelter immediately."

2) If shelter is too far away, get in your vehicle, buckle your seatbelt, and drive away as quickly as possible to the closest sturdy shelter. You must know the direction of the storm![41] If you can "tell pretty confidently what way the tornado is moving, you should try to move at a ninety-degree angle away from it to avoid it," Gallus says. Avoid its path. Forbes adds, "If the tornado is at a distance, stop and let it pass or try to drive away from it if time and roads permit. If it's behind you, don't try to outrun it." Never try to outrun a tornado in urban or congested areas in a car or truck, either. Instead, leave the vehicle immediately for

39   HTTP://www.ready.gov
40   Greg Forbes
41   ibid

safe shelter. If you see a house, get inside it.[42]

3) If you cannot outrun the storm and debris hits your car, pull over and park.[43] "Do not try to shelter under bridges," warns Edwards, "which can create deadly traffic hazards while offering little protection against flying debris." You are safer in a low, flat location.[44]

4) At this point you have two options: Stay in the car or get out. Edwards says, "Vehicles are extremely risky in a tornado. There is no safe option when caught in a tornado in a car, just slightly less-dangerous ones."

If you stay in: put your head down below the windows. Leave your seatbelt on. Cover your head with your hands. If you have a blanket, use that as well.[45]

If you get out: get to "a ditch or culvert, or as close as you can get to being underground," says Gallus. You need to be lower than the road. Lie down and cover your head with your hands. "Try not to be downwind of the car," because there's a big possibility that "it will be picked up and tossed toward you."[46]

Most tornado deaths are caused by flying debris. Protect your head and neck as much as you can. Having a blanket or pillow in the car can be handy for such a time.[47]

After the Storm

"We could hear our neighbors, women and men alike screaming in despair, and children crying out for help." — Diane Humphrey

Injury may result from the direct impact of a tornado, or it may occur afterward when people walk among debris

---

42   ibid
43   William Edwards
44   ibid
45   ibid
46   William Gallus
47   ibid

and enter damaged buildings. A study of injuries after a tornado in Marion, Illinois, showed that fifty percent of the tornado-related injuries were suffered during rescue attempts, cleanup, and other post-tornado activities. Nearly a third of the injuries resulted from stepping on nails. Because tornadoes often damage power lines, gas lines or electrical systems, there is a risk of fire, electrocution, or an explosion. Protecting yourself and your family requires promptly treating any injuries suffered during the storm and using extreme care to avoid further hazards.[48]

Don't leave your safe room until you know the danger is over.[49] Professor Gallus says, "If you know the tornado has hit you, I'd say it is safe to leave within about two or three minutes of hearing the winds die down. If you don't know that the tornado has hit or passed, you should have a radio or weather radio so you can tell when the warning expires, and then you can leave." It's very unlikely that the same tornado will turn around and come back. "They don't really do that," he says. "They just wobble a bit from side to side as they travel in a basically straight line or a slightly arcing line." He admits that it is possible for the storm to "drop another tornado near the original tornado. When this happens, it is usually around the time the first tornado is dying. So, it is always a good idea after leaving a shelter to keep an eye on the sky and listen for weather bulletins in case another tornado touches down. It would be very very rare, though, to witness this happening. Usually the new tornado touches down more like a mile or so away from the other one."

Once you're certain it's safe to leave, he says to "check to see if you have obvious serious injuries, and if you still have shoes on. Look around for nails, glass, and other things to avoid. Make note of gas smells and try to get away from damaged/destroyed houses where you detect the smell." Edwards adds to "keep your family together

48   HTTP://www.ready.gov/tornadoes
49   William Gallus

and wait for emergency personnel to arrive." If you've been separated from family or loved ones, Gallus says you should "try talking to any police, or calling hospitals or just going there."

If you are injured, "in a perfect world, waiting for trained medical people is best, and if the tornado seems kind of small, that should work," Gallus says. "But if [the tornado] is major (like Joplin), you may have no choice but to get yourself to the hospital." Be familiar with basic first-aid skills such as making a tourniquet.[50]

Even if you are uninjured, you will likely encounter others who are. While it's true that you shouldn't attempt to move seriously injured people unless they are in immediate danger of further injury, Gallus also says, "If you are pretty sure you have no injuries and you do have shoes on, I think you should next carefully try to help save other people who will likely be hurt or trapped. If you have access to a cell phone, probably calling 911 is good to let them know exactly where you are and the damage you see, so they can send help. Of course, keep in mind normal medical concerns such as the need to be careful with people who might have broken backs or necks."

In an emergency situation, every helping hand is a saving hand. "Carefully render aid to those who are injured," Edwards says. "Do not use matches or lighters, in case of leaking natural gas pipes or fuel tanks nearby. Remain calm and alert, and listen for information and instructions from emergency crews or local officials. Damage areas are full of hazardous booby traps for survivors. Electric lines might still be charged and must be avoided, along with any puddles or water touching wires. Tripping hazards exists everywhere with debris. Nails, sharp metal objects, and broken glass are common on the ground and embedded in debris piles. Severe infections can occur from being punctured or cut in damage areas, where toilet pipes and other sources of germs have been blasted apart. Stay out

50   ibid

of any heavily damaged houses or buildings; they could collapse at any time." If someone has stopped breathing, begin CPR if you are trained to do so. Stop a bleeding injury by applying direct pressure to the wound.[51] Edwards adds that "Smart-phone apps exist to help with basic first aid. Every storm shelter should contain first-aid kits. The American Red Cross is a great resource to learn both basic first aid and CPR." Have any puncture wound evaluated by a physician.[52]

Sometimes, getting to a physician or hospital might be the hard part. Gallus points out, "As Joplin showed, you can't count on there being enough ambulances." He personally believes you should "try to transport injured to the hospital, or find someone with a working vehicle that could." If you are trapped, try to attract attention to your location.[53]

Here are some safety precautions that could help you avoid injury after a tornado:

Continue to monitor your battery-powered radio or television for emergency information.

Be careful when entering any structure that has been damaged.

Wear sturdy shoes or boots, long sleeves and gloves when handling or walking on or near debris.

Be aware of hazards from exposed nails and broken glass.

Do not touch downed power lines or objects in contact with downed lines. Report electrical hazards to the police and the utility company.

Use battery-powered lanterns, if possible, rather than candles to light homes without electrical power. If you use candles, make sure they are in safe holders away from curtains, paper, wood or other flammable items. Never leave a candle burning when you are out of the room.

51   Roger Edwards
52   ibid
53   HTTP://www.ready.gov/tornadoes

Never use generators, pressure washers, grills, camp stoves or other gasoline, propane, natural gas or charcoal-burning devices inside your home, basement, garage or camper — or even outside near an open window, door or vent. Carbon monoxide (CO) — an odorless, colorless gas that can cause sudden illness and death if you breathe it — from these sources can build up in your home, garage or camper, and poison the people and animals inside. Seek prompt medical attention if you suspect CO poisoning and are feeling dizzy, lightheaded or nauseated.

Hang up displaced telephone receivers that may have been knocked off by the tornado, but stay off the telephone, except to report an emergency.

Cooperate fully with public safety officials.

Respond to requests for volunteer assistance by police, fire fighters, emergency management, and relief organizations, but do not go into damaged areas unless assistance has been requested. Your presence could hamper relief efforts and you could endanger yourself.[54]

Inspecting the Damage

After a tornado, be aware of possible structural, electrical, or gas-leak hazards in your home. Contact your local city or county building inspectors for information on structural safety codes and standards. They may also offer suggestions on finding a qualified contractor to do work for you.[55]

In general, if you suspect any damage to your home, shut off electrical power, natural gas and propane tanks to avoid fire, electrocution or explosions.

If it is dark when you are inspecting your home, use a flashlight rather than a candle or torch to avoid the risk of fire or explosion in a damaged home.

If you see frayed wiring or sparks, or if there is an odor of something burning, you should immediately shut off the

54   ibid
55   ibid

electrical system at the main circuit breaker if you have not done so already.

If you smell gas or suspect a leak, turn off the main gas valve, open all windows, and leave the house immediately. Notify the gas company, the police or fire departments, or State Fire Marshal's office and do not turn on the lights, light matches, smoke, or do anything that could cause a spark. Do not return to your house until you are told it is safe to do so.[56]

If your home has been compromised, you should seek shelter and safety elsewhere. The inclement weather might not be over, and you don't want to be caught in it.[57] "Go to a friend or family member," Gallus says. "Tornadoes are almost never more than one mile wide, so usually you don't have to go too far to find someone who will have a safe place."

Safety During Cleanup

Wear sturdy shoes or boots, long sleeves and gloves.

Learn proper safety procedures and operating instructions before operating any gas-powered or electric-powered saws or tools.

Clean up spilled medicines, drugs, flammable liquids and other potentially hazardous materials.[58]

Recommended Supplies to Include in a Basic Kit (as provided by FEMA):

– Water, one gallon of water per person per day, for drinking and sanitation. You can store water in old juice bottles, soda bottles, and water bottles.

– Food, at least a three-day supply of non-perishable food.

– Battery-powered radio and a NOAA Weather Radio with tone alert, and extra batteries for both.

– Flashlight and extra batteries.

56   ibid
57   William Gallus
58   HTTP://www.ready.gov/tornadoes

- First-aid kit.
- Whistle to signal for help.
- Infant formula and diapers, if you have an infant. (Don't assume you'll be able to nurse. Stress and lack of food could impact your milk supply.)
- Moist towelettes, garbage bags and plastic ties for personal sanitation.
- Dust mask or cotton T-shirt, to help filter the air.
- Plastic sheeting and duct tape to shelter-in-place.
- Wrench or pliers to turn off utilities.
- Can opener for food (if kit contains canned food).[59]
Clothing and Bedding:
If you live in a cold weather climate, you must think about warmth. It is possible that the power will be out and you will not have heat. Rethink your clothing and bedding supplies to account for growing children and other family changes. One complete change of warm clothing and shoes per person, including:
- A jacket or coat
- Long pants
- A long sleeved shirt
- Sturdy shoes
- A hat and gloves
- A sleeping bag or warm blanket for each person[60]
Below are some other items for your family to consider adding to its supply kit. Some of these items, especially those marked with an *, can be dangerous, so please have an adult collect these supplies.
- Emergency reference materials such as a first-aid book or a printout of the information on www.ready.gov
- Rain gear
- Mess kits, paper cups, plates and plastic utensils
- Cash or travelers checks, change
- Paper towels
- Fire Extinguisher

59   ibid
60   ibid

- Tent
- Compass
- Matches in a waterproof container*
- Signal flare*
- Paper, pencil
- Personal hygiene items including feminine supplies
- Disinfectant*

–Household chlorine bleach* — You can use bleach as a disinfectant (diluted nine parts water to one part bleach), or in an emergency you can also use it to treat water. Use 16 drops of regular household liquid bleach per gallon of water. Do not use scented, color-safe, or bleaches with added cleaners.

- Medicine dropper

–Important Family Documents such as copies of insurance policies, identification and bank account records in a waterproof, portable container[61]

---

61   HTTP://www.ready.gov/tornadoes

Glossary

Area of Low Pressure: a region where the atmospheric pressure is lower than that of surrounding locations

Cold Front: the zone separating two air masses, of which the cooler, denser mass is advancing and replacing the warmer

Convective Available Potential Energy (CAPE): the amount of energy a parcel of air would have if lifted a certain distance vertically through the atmosphere

Cumulus: a group of clouds characterized by dense individual elements in the form of puffs, mounds, or towers, with flat bases and tops that often resemble cauliflower

Degrees of Damage (DOD): the amount of damage caused by wind

Emergency Kit: a package of basic tools and supplies prepared in advance as an aid to survival in an emergency

Enhanced F-Scale: rates the strength of tornadoes in the United States based on the damage they cause, revised from the Fujita Scale to reflect better examinations of tornado damage surveys

Fujita Scale: a scale for rating tornado intensity, based primarily on the damage tornadoes inflict on human-built structures and vegetation

Funnel Cloud: a rapidly rotating funnel-shaped cloud extending downward from the base of a cumulonimbus cloud

Gale: a wind of 32-63 mph

Hodograph: a diagram that gives the visual representation of the movement of a body or a fluid

Jet Stream: strong, generally westerly winds concentrated in a relatively narrow and shallow stream in the upper troposphere of the earth

236

Knot: one nautical mile per hour, approximately 1.15 miles per hour

Local Storm Report (LSR): a report transmitted by the National Weather Service, used to issue Severe Thunderstorm Warnings, Tornado Warnings, and other weather warnings/bulletins

Mesocyclone: a small cyclone that arises near a thunderstorm and is sometimes associated with the occurrence of tornadoes

Meteorological: pertaining to phenomena of the atmosphere or weather

Meteorologist: one who studies meteorology

Millibar: A unit of pressure used to measure air pressure; equal to one thousandth of a bar or 1000 dynes per square centimeter

NOAA Weather Radio: a network of radio stations broadcasting continuous weather information directly from a nearby National Weather Service (NWS) office

Optimism Bias: a bias that causes a person to believe that they are less at risk of experiencing a negative event compared to others

PathCast: a system that calculates the direct path of the tornado and create a warning for those in the direct projectory

Radar: a device for determining the presence and location of an object by measuring the time for the echo of a radio wave to return from it and the direction from which it returns

Safe Room: a fortified room which is installed in a private residence or business to provide a safe shelter, or hiding place, for the inhabitants in the event of a tornado or other threat

Storm Prediction Center (SPC): located in Norman, Oklahoma, SPC is tasked with forecasting the risk of severe thunderstorms and tornadoes in the contiguous United States

Supercell: A thunderstorm with a persistent rotating

updraft

Surface Low: the pressure measured by a barometer at the surface is lower than the areas around it

Thunderstorm: a moving storm of lightning and thunder, usually with rain and gusty winds, sometimes with hail; produced by cumulonimbus clouds

Tornado: a violently destructive windstorm occurring over land and characterized by a long, funnel-shaped cloud extending toward the ground and made visible by condensation and debris

Troposphere: the lowest layer of the atmosphere, within which nearly all cloud formations occur and weather conditions manifest themselves

Vortex: a whirling mass of air, especially one in the form of a visible column or spiral

WarnGen System: a system that sends the Tornado Warning out to all cities and towns that could possibly be in the vicinity of the tornado

Weather Forecast Office (WFO): local branches of the National Weather Service

Wind Fields: the three-dimensional spatial pattern of winds

About the Author

Tamara Hart Heiner lives in Arkansas with her husband and soon-to-be four children. She graduated from Brigham Young University with a degree in English. She is the author of the young adult suspense novels **Perilous**, **Altercation**, and **Inevitable**. Besides writing, she enjoys all things food, especially baking. Perhaps someday she'll own a bakery and sell her own books inside.

http://tamarahartheiner.com
http://tamarahartheiner.blogspot.com

CPSIA information can be obtained
at www.ICGtesting.com
Printed in the USA
FFOW03n2103050518
46442110-48332FF